Workplace Prayers

Daily Strength and Wisdom

Dr. Wendy J. Flint

Word Unlimited Publishing
Since 1985
Vancouver, WA - Indio, CA - Temple, TX
Portland, OR
PO Box Updated @ **www.drwendyflint.com**

Workplace Prayers

Daily Strength and Wisdom

USA ISBN 978-0-9818470-1-6
Word Unlimited

"Let your heart retain my words; keep my commands, and live. Get wisdom! Get understanding! Do not forget, nor turn away from the words of my mouth. Do not forsake her [wisdom], and she will preserve you; love her, and she will keep you. Wisdom is the principal thing; therefore get wisdom. And in all your getting, get understanding. Exalt her, and she will promote you; She will bring you honor, when you embrace her. She will place on your head an ornament of grace; a crown of glory she will deliver to you" (Proverbs 4: 4- 9).

Dedication

I dedicate this book to my sisters-in-Christ who prayed for me the past 20 to 40 years – Lorinda, Anita, Pam, Sherry, and Bev. And to my daughter Tracy who always gives me a God-inspired encouraging word. Thank you for listening to all my workplace stories.

In Memory

Reverend Michael Moreland who passed suddenly on February 22, 2015. He was my pastor for two years before he retired at St. Andrew Presbyterian Church in Indio, CA. He read my marketplace devotions every day and wrote:

"I wanted to be sure and say thank you for your Godly insights, study, and regard for scripture. Keep up the good work. I am sure you have a nice devotional book in the making that will be of great value to believers in the secular workplace and those like me working in the church."

Table of Contents

Introduction by Dr. Wendy Flint

The Lord impressed on my heart many years ago that I would have a "Fruits of the Spirit Ministry." I had a vision of grapes and in studying the vision, I realized that the "new wine" that must be poured through our lives out to others can only be accomplished through a "crushing." As Apostle Paul would say, "we are crushed so that we can be poured out to others – so that the glory of God is revealed in us" (Philippians 2:17).

Jesus said that "new wine" could not be poured into old wineskins or it would burst (Matthew 9:16-18). That is why our vessel is always going through a renewal from "glory to glory" until we reflect our Maker.

Jesus also said that He is the Vine and we are the branches, and we can accomplish nothing without Him (John 15:5). We must abide in Him for the fruit to be produced.

The fruits are love, joy, peace, longsuffering [patience], kindness, goodness, faithfulness, gentleness, and self-control" (Galatians 5: 22 & 23).

The only way these fruits can be developed is through pressure. Our true character is revealed under pressure. The pressure is ongoing and always changing because we are always growing and changing. Like wine becoming better with time, we become better with the pressures of life because we learn to trust God more with each situation.

I have worked for two organizations in Napa, California. I have had an opportunity to talk to wine makers and view the beautiful vineyards. I discovered that some vines are good at bearing fruit, but others are not. Often the non-producing vine becomes "root stock." Certain root stocks have been identified as having a natural ability to fight off disease.

The fruit-bearing branches are grafted into the root stock. The root stock does not produce any fruit of its own – but it provides all the nourishment and protection that the grafted grape vines need.

How clear it all becomes that Jesus, "the root vine," needs us – the branches – to produce fruit for Him in this world. But if we don't graft ourselves in – abide in Him – the strength and nourishment will not flow, and we may dry up, succumb to disease, and become fruitless – producing nothing for Him.

The Lord is telling me through the vineyard example that I cannot produce fruit of myself. I cannot walk in perfect love, joy, peace, patience, goodness, kindness, gentleness, faithfulness, or self-control in the workplace, home, church, or community *without Him*.

As Jesus inspires and encourages me with messages, I write them for Christians in the workplace, so that His Spirit, the Holy Spirit, can strengthen my brothers and sisters through His Word.

Yet, it is not enough. You will have to spend time in His Word and do your own abiding to produce the fruit you need to be victorious and prepare for eternity.

Preface

In 2010, I was required to travel by flight every week for an executive sales job. As soon as the plane would reach 30,000 feet, the Holy Spirit would birth a prayer in my spirit and I would find a scripture to go with it. As a writer, I always traveled with a journal. Five or six prayers would rapidly flow from my pen then stop. This continued on 20 roundtrips (40 flights) until I had 200 prayers.

This book is more needed now than ever before in the history of workplace America. Christians are enduring persecution, ethical dilemmas, lawsuits and incompetent leadership in greed-driven organizations.

Yet, in the worst of companies, God wants to be Lord and He does that through us.

One scripture and prayer a day can make a huge difference in accessing the wisdom and strength we need to stand strong and to let peace prevail.

Corporations, hospitals, governments, and schools are high-pressured and stress-filled, but if we abide in Him through His Word and a moment of prayer, He will abide in us.

✍ Workplace Wisdom

Also included in this book are Workplace Wisdom devotionals that were written in journal and then sent by email daily to over 1000 Christians throughout the United States.

Here are some comments about the messages:

"Wow! You have outdone yourself with this one. I'm going to print this message and have it tattooed on my forehead. Thanks for the great insights. Your daily devotions frequently move me. They speak to my soul in a language that transcends the written or spoken word."

Miles, Retired Police Captain, California

"What a POWERFUL message from the Lord – one which we can all follow. Thank you for sharing with us and helping all of us to hear Him and understand Him. Your faithfulness is precious. It is so comforting to have a woman as a Christian professional role-model and spiritual guide. Keep the words coming!"

Monica, Pottery Barn Manager, California

"Wow! Powerful devotion today. Great insight. I had tears in my eyes as I read. I was touched. Thanks for sending them. They're great."

Ben, Campus Crusade for Christ, Florida

Daily Prayer # 1

"Blessed is the man who does not walk in the counsel of the wicked or stand in the way of sinners or sit in the seat of mockers. But his delight is in the law of the Lord, and on His law he meditates day and night. He is like a tree planted by streams of water, which yields its fruit in season and whose leaf does not wither. Whatever he does prospers." Psalms 1: 1 - 3

Lord – I will avoid sinners, mockers and scoffers. I will delight in Your word and meditate on it every day. I know if I do, I will produce fruit in a dry season and like the tree by the river, I will not wither or age. I will be strong – yet I will be flexible in times of change. According to your promise – whatever I do shall prosper. I will seek out those who care about righteous living and serving You.

Daily Prayer # 2

"You will not fear the terror of the night, nor the arrow that flies by day, nor the pestilence that stalks in the darkness, nor the plague that destroys at midday. A thousand may fall at you side, ten thousand at your right hand, but it will not come near you." Psalm 91: 5 – 7

Lord – According to Your word – 1000 can be sick 10,000 have a flu virus – but it will not come near me. If I temporarily have no provision, I live with joy in your economy, not the world's economy. It is time for me to listen and yield to your promises and not yield to the fears and voices of those around me or in the news. I choose to trust You and You alone.

Daily Prayer # 3

"What He opens no one can shut, and what he shuts no one can open. I know your deeds. See, I have placed before you an open door that no one can shut." Revelation 3: 7 – 8

Lord – I know you are watching over my journey and path. All my steps will lead to You and to Your will for my life. I know that your hand is upon me and You will finish what you have begun. You will open doors for me that Satan cannot shut. You have always prepared a place for me in the presence of my enemies. As I look back at all you have done for me – I am overwhelmed. My cup is full. Let Your love for me overflow to others today.

Daily Prayer # 4

"Trust in the Lord and do good; dwell in the land and enjoy safe pasture." Psalms 37: 3

Lord – I will keep my hope in You. Those with no hope, experience despair; but those who trust You will enter the promise land of provision, health and safety. I choose to not be like the Israelites who feared, complained, and stayed in the wilderness until death. I choose to cross over into the land of plenty by only speaking and praying Your promises. Put a guard on my tongue and cause me to always remember the power of my words.

Daily Prayer # 5

"Delight yourself in the Lord and he will give you the desires of your heart." Psalms 37: 4

Lord – Your word says "delight yourself." That means I have to choose to delight in my thoughts and emotions. Delight means to "behold with great appreciation." It means to "think of with joy, appreciate the wonderfulness, and to be happy and content with yourself." I delight in who I am, the person You created; and I delight in the gifts you have given me. I delight in my salvation and in Jesus Christ my Lord. I am delighted with my family – the heritage of the Lord. Thank you for giving me the desires of my heart.

Daily Prayer # 6

"Go and enjoy choice food and sweet drinks, and send some to those who have nothing prepared. This day is sacred to our Lord. Do not grieve, for the joy of the Lord is your strength." Nehemiah 8: 10

Lord – I choose to smile today. I choose to be thankful and happy. Even if I have trials, I will look to the needs of others. I will think of your blessings with joy and in that joy will be my strength. In that strength I will be able to do all the tasks you have for me today and endure the unhappiness or anger of others. Let me be a cup of cold water of joy in a very parched land.

Daily Prayer # 7

"May the words of my mouth and the meditation of my heart be pleasing in your sight, O LORD, my Rock and my Redeemer." Psalm 19: 14

Lord –I don't want the words of my mouth to discourage or hurt others. I want to encourage and be a source of healing. How sad we must make You when we speak words of fear and complaint. How You long for our words to speak faith so that we can create a garden of beauty around us. Help me not to plant weeds in my garden because they can take over the beauty and faith that You desire for me. Put a guard on my mouth today and let my words be pleasing to You.

Daily Prayer # 8

"I will give you every place where you set your foot, as I promised Moses. Be strong and courageous, because you will lead these people to inherit the land I swore to their forefathers to give them. Be careful to obey all the law my servant Moses gave you; do not turn from it to the right or to the left, that you may be successful wherever you go" Joshua 1: 3 – 10

Lord – I know if I walk a crooked path of ungodly behavior and do not obey Your word, I will not prosper and I will be miserable. Prosper does not mean just finances- it means protection and health for me and my loved ones. With Your help, I choose to not step to the left with profane or crude language, gossip, or words of unbelief. Rather, I will speak Your word and things that edify others. With your help, I will not step to the right and compromise my thoughts or actions under stress or pressure. Rather, I will walk in the straight path of love, forgiveness, and kindness.

Daily Prayer # 9

"Jabez cried out to the God of Israel, 'Oh that you would bless me and enlarge my territory! Let your hand be with me, and keep me from harm so that I will be free from pain.' And God granted his request." I Chronicles 4: 10

Lord – I used to pray that You will bless the work of my hands that I may prosper; but what I should pray is "use me to bless others in a mighty way." Expand my thinking, expand my vision, expand my prayers so that You can expand my territory and in turn expand Your Kingdom here on earth.

Daily Prayer # 10

"Now to him who is able to do immeasurably more than all we ask or imagine, according to his power that is at work within us" Ephesians 3: 20

Lord – If this is my "destiny" to be in this place for a short time or long time – then please let it be more than just counting the days. I want to be part of something that creates opportunity and purpose for others. I want to make a difference in the world. I want to bloom where I am planted. Let the things that I do impact others around me and let it be a contributing factor to something bigger than just me and my tasks. I am expecting big things – more than I can ask or imagine. Thank you.

 Workplace Wisdom

Don't Give Up

In 2008, I went on a 21-day fast to receive a revelation about my ministry and to pray for my family.

Several days past the 21-day mark, I continued to pray, waiting on the Lord. On day 25, I was on an airplane heading from Texas to our home in California. As I sat in the coach class of the plane, my heart was a little heavy because there was no clear revelation.

I sat with my eyes closed, and then I heard, "Ms. Flint, are you Ms. Flint? Please come with me, you've been upgraded to first class."

Since my new seat was in bulkhead, I could not put anything on the floor in front of me, so I grabbed my Bible, my journal, and a pen. Just as I got settled and looked out the window, I received a revelation in my spirit from the Lord and quickly wrote it down as it came to me:

"I saw your 21-day fast. I heard your heart ask the question, 'Why was there no revelation?'

My answer is, 'How do you know I will not come on day 22, 23, 24, or 25?' You don't know – so don't ever give up. Seek Me until you receive the answer. You chose 21-days because it took that long for the messenger angel to get to Daniel when he prayed, but you must seek Me for as many days as it takes."

The Lord went on to say to my heart as clear as if He was sitting there next to me:

"What is it to you if I show up on day 45 – does it matter? What are 45 days in all eternity? How undisciplined and impatient My people are. I am pleased that on day 25 you are still seeking Me – waiting on Me – serving Me.

"I know you have prayed 35 years for members of your family. What are 36, 37, 38, or 40 years to the Lord if I have an appointed time? What does it matter if they are spared in year 45 of prayer as long as they come into the will of God?

"How do you know if it will not be year 45 that the bondage and chains are broken? You don't know – so you must be faithful and keep praying.

"What you *DO* know is MY WORD, and My Word is true. I am a faithful God and My Word says "your entire household shall be saved" (Joshua 24:15).

I sat there in awe – silent in the presence of God – as the plane lifted into the sky. Then the woman next to me, who saw my Bible, said, "Are you a Christian? So am I." She had also been selected to be upgraded to first class.

In the conversation and fellowship, she shared how she had recently been born-again and how within a year, every single person in her family was saved, from her mother, to her husband, to her children. God wanted to say to me in that exact moment – on day 25 – "See – I told you I can save a whole family – don't give up."

(Note: This was written in 2008. In 2013, my 93-year-old mother accepted the Lord after 40 years of prayer.)

Daily Prayer # 11

"God gave Solomon wisdom and very great insight, and a breadth of understanding as measureless as the sand on the seashore." I Kings 4: 29

Lord – We are surrounded by people in rebellion. They are immoral, lack work ethic, profane your name, and lust after things of the world. Your truth and wisdom is within us. We have a light to offer a lost world. I ask you to let Your wisdom come forth through me. Let the decisions I make and the problems I solve be profound in the eyes of those who walk the wrong path. Let wisdom radiate from me so that others will be drawn to your love and power. Use me as you used Solomon, Joseph, Daniel, Nehemiah, and Esther. Let my leadership skills become the platform that will be able to give God the glory.

Daily Prayer # 12

"But blessed is the man who trusts in the LORD, whose confidence is in him." Jeremiah 17: 7

Lord – Is there a seat you want me to take? Perhaps the seat of a new job, the seat of leadership, the seat of teaching a Bible study, or the seat of going back to school? You have built my confidence, oh Lord, and you will equip me for the tasks before me. If you open the door, provide the way, and give me the skills and resources, I will take the seat. Give me the courage and the confidence to move to higher levels. With God on my side, all things are possible. Use me to advance the Kingdom of Heaven where I am seated.

Daily Prayer # 13

"Christ redeemed us from the curse of the law by becoming a curse for us, for it is written: 'Cursed is everyone who is hung on a tree.' He redeemed us in order that the blessing given to Abraham might come to the Gentiles through Christ Jesus, so that by faith we might receive the promise of the Spirit." Galatians 3: 13 & 14

Lord – According to Your word I am blessed and not cursed. I walk in the blessing of Noah and Abraham because of Jesus Christ. Bless me in my marriage, bless me in my work, bless my children, bless my grandchildren, and bless my animals. I ask a special blessing on those around me. May all cursing that comes against me be consumed in the love of Jesus and fall to the earth unfruitful. I receive Your blessing today and always.

Daily Prayer # 14

"Before I formed you in the womb I knew you, before you were born I set you apart; I appointed you as a prophet to the nations." Jeremiah 1: 5

Lord – If possible, I have a special request. Please call together and thank all those that have gone before us. Thank those who fought the good fight to pray for this nation, thank those who persevered to invent the things we enjoy today, thank those who created businesses that employ Your people. Thank those who paid a price in war to give us our freedom. Thank those who were persecuted in political offices standing for justice and moral values. Thank the pastors who spiritually guide us and built churches to train us. Thank the writers and speakers who have inspired and strengthened us. Now Lord I ask, let me be one who creates benefits and blessings for future generations. Set me apart to do great things for You.

Daily Prayer # 15

"But I will establish my covenant with you, and you will enter the ark – you and your sons and your wife and your sons' wives with you." Genesis 6: 1

Lord – What a powerful word you spoke to Noah – *establish*. It means firm and stable – not wavering. I want to be established not unstable or changing on a whim. I want my emotions to be steady and peace to rule my heart and mind. Establish me, establish my finances, establish my family, establish my future, establish my gifts and talents, establish my marriage, and establish my ministry. You are an establishing God and I believe in Your ability to finish what you began in my life.

Daily Prayer # 16

"The Scripture foresaw that God would justify the Gentiles by faith, and announced the gospel in advance to Abraham: 'All nations will be blessed through you.' So those who have faith are blessed along with Abraham, the man of faith." Galatians 3: 8 & 9

Lord – By Your grace and favor and according to Your word, bless everything I put my hand to. Bless every person I talk to, every friend and loved one I pray for, every letter I write, every leader I report to, and bless this nation. Thank you for passing this blessing on to me and my family through Jesus Christ our Lord.

Daily Prayer # 17

"Not that I have already obtained all this, or have already been made perfect, but I press on to take hold of that for which Christ Jesus took hold of me. Brothers [and Sisters], I do not consider myself yet to have taken hold of it. But one thing I do: Forgetting what is behind and straining toward what is ahead. I press on toward the goal to win the prize for which God has called me heavenward in Christ Jesus." Philippians 3: 12 – 14

Lord – Keep me focused on the things I need to accomplish today. A pilot in a jet can only look forward and look to the left and the right. It is impossible for a pilot to look back as they thrust forward at 500 to 800 miles per hour. Help me to stay alert to attacks that could come from the left or right – and to keep my eye on the mission, the destination, and on You. Remind me that others are on the plane and I am leading them to a destination also. I will not look back at the mistakes and failures of me or others – but only look forward to new beginnings without regret.

Daily Prayer # 18

"You are all sons and daughters of God through faith in Christ Jesus, for all of you who were baptized into Christ have clothed yourselves with Christ." Galatians 3: 26

Lord – I want people to call me by *Your Name*. I want them to see Jesus in me. I want people to respect the goodness of the Lord and know that they can receive God's love and blessing just as You have blessed me. I need you to do that through me because I cannot make that happen. I know as I abide in You – You will abide in me and you can make Yourself known to others. You are a great God. Please be a great God through me to others.

Daily Prayer # 19

"Now Daniel so distinguished himself among the administrators and the satraps (supervisors) by his exceptional qualities that the king planned to set him over the whole kingdom." Daniel 6: 3

Lord – Pursuing excellence, following the teachings of Jesus, and walking in love takes diligence, time, courage, willingness, and sometimes toughness. This may be "easy" for high achieving personality types, but for many, it is a daily battle. Does this walking and working toward perfection really matter? I hear You saying in my spirit, "don't throw in the towel yet – because it does!" Help me to not give up and to not take the easy, wide road. Help me to remember that my work is eternal and that all of this is a training ground for eternal purposes.

Daily Prayer # 20

"I tell you the truth, unless a kernel of wheat falls to the ground and dies, it remains only a single seed. But if it dies, it produces many seeds." John 12: 24

Lord – Thank you that farmers do not till the ground forever and neither do You. There is a time for seed planting and a time for the harvest. I know that whatever I go through, it is only for a season. After my heart is soft and pliable, you will plant and produce a new crop of success out of my failures. It is then and only then that I can give you all the glory for my accomplishments. Remind me that the word of God is the seed and the watering is the praise, worship, and a spirit of thankfulness. With the Holy Spirit's help, I will praise You through all stages from tilling, to planting, to harvesting. Keep Satan from stealing my joy in the process or destroying my crop in its fullness.

✍ Workplace Wisdom

Good Success

"Moses My servant is dead. Now therefore, arise, go over this Jordan, you and all this people, to the land which I am giving to them – the children of Israel." Joshua 1: 1

I love the book of Joshua. This is a man that was willing to face the giants with Caleb when everyone else was too fearful. When his time finally came to lead (40 years later) after Moses died, God told him to be strong and courageous and know that God was with him as He was with Moses (verse 5). John Maxwell wrote: "It took 40 years for Joshua's leadership style to match the need of the moment." (Maxwell's Leadership Bible). The moment called for a much more confrontational leader, skilled in warfare.

Joshua knew how to have good success. I discovered his successful leadership guidelines in his behaviors and God's promises:

1) Expect God's favor when your ways please him (Joshua 2: 8 – 11, 24; 3: 7).
2) Practice scripture memorization and meditation and put it into practice (Joshua 1: 7 & 8).
3) Keep a record of experiences (Joshua4: 4 - 7).
4) Do not do not covet this world's goods or adopt this world's way of thinking and behavior (Joshua 2: 3 & 7).
5) Rely on God's strength and wisdom (Joshua 1: 6).

6) Seek the Lord prayerfully for every decision (Joshua 9: 14).
7) Believe God's promises (Joshua 21:45; 23: 14).
8) Be assured that He will never forsake you. (Joshua 17: 18).

Good success does not mean there will not be any tests and trials – it means God's favor will be in the midst of our trials. Good success means accomplishing God's will for our lives. It means reaching our vision and destiny.

Don't get weary in staying on track with God's law or the things listed above for good success. If you feel you have been stuck in a trial or wilderness for too long – stop and get some clarity. Write down your successes as you evaluate where you have come from and make a new list of where you need to be headed. Start moving in that direction. Start practicing you dream right where you are at, using your gifts and talents, and watch for an open door.

Daily Prayer # 21

"I planted the seed, Apollos watered it, but God made it grow. So neither he who plants nor he who waters is anything, but only God, who makes things grow. The man who plants and the man who waters have one purpose, and each will be rewarded according to his own labor." I Corinthians 3: 6 – 7

Lord –Help me to be a seed planter and know that it is just as important as the harvest. For those that have hard hearts, help me to do my best to plant seeds of wisdom and water them with prayer. Help me to set a good example and to model your love. Help me to reflect the fruits of the Spirit in all circumstances. When a door of opportunity opens, give me the courage to share my testimony and gratitude for a loving God. Whenever possible, I will plant seeds of joy, peace, and thanksgiving.

Daily Prayer # 22

"Jesus called them together and said, "You know that the rulers of the Gentiles lord it over them, and their high officials exercise authority over them. Not so with you. Instead, whoever wants to become great among you must be your servant and whoever wants to be first must be your slave – just as the Son of Man did not come to be served, but to serve, and to give his life as ransom for many." Matthew 20: 24 – 27

Lord – Fill me with your servant attitude today and provide opportunities for me to do something for someone else that will make a difference in his or her life. When I am successful, remind me of my humble beginnings and to treat everyone as an equal. May Jesus manifest Himself through me in all situations.

Daily Prayer # 23

"Blessed is the man or woman who does not walk in the counsel of the wicked or stand in the way of sinners or sit in the seat of mockers." Psalms 1:1

Lord –We are in a time where good is called evil and evil is called good. Give me the courage Lord to represent You and not fear what man can do to me. Help me to find the balance between showing your example in action and deed and speaking the truth in boldness. Help me to understand that I am in spiritual authority in places that I walk and that through prayer I will not let Satan rule me or my environment. Don't let me be silent Lord when I should speak and don't let me speak when I should be silent. Help me to be joyful and positive and to create images of strength, peace, and maturity.

Daily Prayer # 24

"Consequently, faith comes from hearing the message, and the message is heard through the word of Christ." Romans 10: 17

Lord –Always remind me that my faith will not exceed the knowledge of Your Word. If I don't meditate on Your Word – how will I know Your promises? How will I face the fears of this age? My faith will not be any higher than the level of my confession and my confession will not be any higher than the meditation of my heart on Your word. I will believe what I speak. Help me to speak Your promises today and not listen to the voices of doubt, lies, fear, or unbelief.

Daily Prayer # 25

"But if we walk in the light, as He is in the light, we have fellowship with one another, and the blood of Jesus, his Son, purifies us from all sin." I John 1: 7

Lord –We need each other to be successful. I will make an effort to reach out to others to share ideas and learn new things. I will look for opportunities to encourage others and pray when appropriate. I need other Christians as much as they need me to survive. Help me to find fellowship in this place.

Daily Prayer # 26

"The tongue has the power of life and death, and those who love it will eat its fruit." Proverbs 18: 21

Lord – If bitterness, envy, jealousy, anger, or depression is in my heart – then my words will reflect this. I have the power to give life or speak words of death to others. I need wisdom and self-control to always speak what is right and good. I know with prayer and practice the fruits of the Spirit will grow within me. I humble myself before You to confess that I need You to help me walk in Love all the time. It is You in me that will enable me to be kind and have a gentle response. As I abide in you with these Daily Prayers, thank you for abiding in me.

Daily Prayer # 27

"I saw the Lord always before me, because He is at my right hand, I will not be shaken." Acts 2: 25

Lord –If you are an unshakable God and I am created in Your image and likeness, then through Christ, I should be unshakable too. If you are a Rock and our High Tower, then I should not be moved by circumstances. I want to stand strong in my personal battles. I want to not be moved during financial challenges. I want to calmly respond and not be emotionally moved by poor performance or poor behavior of others. The only way I can do that is to have more of You in me. I choose to build my house on the Rock – the Lord Jesus Christ.

Daily Prayer # 28

"Many are the plans in a man's heart, but it is the Lord's purpose that prevails." Proverbs 19: 21

Lord – I think the difference between joy and depression is purpose. With Your guidance let me have a sense of what I was created to do. Help me to know my gifts and talents and how to apply them each and every day; in each circumstance that You bring my way. Direct me to make clear choices that align with who I am in You. Allow me to be satisfied in my work assignments and life. Use me to help others find purpose and give me contentment on my journey, knowing that ultimately our eternal purpose is to meet You and hear You say, "Well done my good and faithful servant."

Daily Prayer # 29

"'For my thoughts are not your thoughts, and neither are your ways my ways,'" declares the Lord." Isaiah 55: 8

Lord – When Your ways do not make sense to me, help me to trust that there is something of higher purpose happening. I must trust that You are on the throne and You are still in control of the master plan. Reveal to me the wisdom You want me to see and the strength and character you are building through my circumstances.

Daily Prayer # 30

"Do not be afraid or discouraged because of this vast army. For the battle is not yours, but God's." II Chronicles 20: 15

Lord – When I lift up my hands to worship in tough situations, I have to turn my back to the enemy and face You. I have to believe that You have my back covered. I have to let go of everything – even drop my weapons of warfare – and know that Your glory will be my rear guard of protection. If I try to face the enemy and fight without prayer and worship, I am putting my back to you. Help me to not rush in and fight my own battles so quickly. Remind me to spend time waiting upon you. As I worship You, I know You will fight my battles for me.

 Workplace Wisdom

More Than We Ask

"For unto Him who is able to exceedingly abundantly do more than we ask or think according to the power that works in us through Jesus Christ Our Lord" (Ephesians 3: 20, Amplified).

God is able to do MORE than we ask or think. When He answers prayer – it is even beyond our hopes, dreams, and imaginations. Not only will He exceedingly and abundantly help us – He will also work His power THROUGH us because Jesus lives within us.

For many years I misunderstood a picture of my life vision that a pastor/evangelist had spoken to me. I thought the pastor said, "The open door God has for your ministry is so big it will seem miles wide and high to you. In actuality, from the Holy Spirit's point of view, He has to get down on his knees to look through a small door to call you into the other side. Once you step through the door, God will provide all the resources you need to do what He has called you to do."

Twenty years later I was reading that message in my journal, and you know what it really said? It said, "From the Holy Spirit's point of view, YOU – Wendy – will have to get down on YOUR hands and knees to go through the door because GOD IN YOU IS BIGGER THAN THE DOOR!!"

In other words, God will have me so equipped and prepared that even if the mission may seem overwhelming – in reality, it will *not* be difficult with God on my side. What a wonderful image of God being BIG in us to do our assigned tasks.

Are you praying for a vision, dream, or mission in your life? Guess what?

- God is exceedingly able to make you debt free.
- God is exceedingly able to provide you with the resources you need.
- God will abundantly give you wisdom and grace.
- God is able to give you all the gifts and talents you need.
- His power within you will give you health and strength.

The creator of the universe is ABLE to complete His plan for your life – beyond what you can ask, think, or imagine.

Do you have an overwhelming project ahead? Write it down and meditate on the promise – God is Able. God is not only able to give you what you need to succeed – He is faithful to His word and He will do it. And remember – He will do it THROUGH YOU.

Are you thinking too small about your life, career, or finances? Allow God to fill your mind and spirit with a new dream and then write the plan down. In that plan, write some baby steps that will get you going toward the right direction.

Daily Prayer # 31

"You are the salt of the earth. But if the salt loses its saltiness, how can it be made salty again? You are the light of the world. A city on a hill cannot be hidden. ...In the same way, let your light shine before men, that they may see your good deeds and praise your Father in heaven." Matthew 5: 13 – 16

Lord – Thank you for reminding me that "seasoned" small acts of love and kindness go a long way in a world of heartache and loneliness. Let me be your hope and light to someone today. If I have not love – then my words and actions have no meaning at all. Let me be a light for You. When others are confused, help me to be confident. When others are under pressure, help me to be peaceful. When others are overwhelmed, help me to help them overcome. When others are short-tempered, help me to forgive.

Daily Prayer # 32

"Therefore I tell you, whatever you ask for in prayer, believe that you have received it, and it will be yours." Mark 11: 24

Lord – You said to ask *and* believe. It is not enough to just ask – but you require us to have faith to know and trust that you want to answer our prayer. It is an agreement between You and me. Remind me to bring the little things to You each day so that the little things do not become a big crisis. I commit this day to You for Your glory. Walk with me and let Your peace be upon me.

Daily Prayer # 33

"Religion that God our Father accepts as pure and faultless is this: to look after orphans and widows in their distress and to keep oneself from being polluted by the world." James 1: 27

Lord – How can I show my love for You? According to Your Word – I must give my life away and give my love away. I must befriend the friendless and share my food with the hungry. In a world of busyness and stress how easy it is to forget how simple it is to serve You. Open my eyes to see where I can give away my life and love on Your behalf.

Daily Prayer # 34

"Is the Lord's arm too short? You will now see whether or not what I say will come true for you." Numbers 11: 23

Lord – May the comfort and hope of Your Holy Spirit touch the lives and hearts of those who are suffering. Let this be a time of strengthening and growing closer to You. Use me to remind people that the last words of Our Lord were, "I will not leave You or forsake you." Remind us each and every day that You will make a way where there seems to be no way.

Daily Prayer # 35

"Don't be afraid of them. Remember the Lord, who is great and awesome, and fight for your brothers, your sons and your daughters, your wives and your homes." Nehemiah 4: 14

Lord – Help me to not shrink back in tough times but to move forward with courage and strength to take the land. I come against fear and laziness and anything that raises itself up against the Name of the Lord. Help me to recognize who I am in Christ. I will put on the armor of God and stand my ground of faith in the days ahead. I pray for heart protection, mind protection, and physical protection. I pray for emotional healing and moral stability and I pray for my whole family to come in under my prayers of projection.

Daily Prayer # 36

"Come to me, all you who are weary and burdened, and I will give you rest." (Jesus) Matthew 11: 28

Lord – In order to reach the purpose you have for me in my lifetime I am going to need more of You. I know I need to abide in You more to demonstrate Your power, peace and joy to others. To overcome weariness, I need to remember that it is all about You and not about me. You said, "All we have to do is ask," Right now I am pausing to ask You to abide in me and let Your strength flow through me. Let every breath I take be full of you. Thank you for taking away the weariness. Let the joy of the Lord be my strength today.

Daily Prayer # 37

"Small is the gate and narrow the road that leads to life, and only a few find it." Matthew 7: 14

Lord – People in this world are chasing after counterfeits instead of a relationship with the one true God. I don't know when and how You are going to turn this around – but I know I need to make sure I am not a counterfeit when others are searching for the path to You. Help me to always know the truth, speak the truth, and reflect the truth in my behaviors. Do not let me be deceived to accept anything less than a truthful and open relationship with You.

Daily Prayer # 38

"Accept one another, then just as Christ accepted you, in order to bring praise to God." Romans 15: 7

Lord – Help us to accept the unique callings and assignments You give each one of us. Help us to remember that unity does not mean everyone thinking and saying the same thing. Unity means a love and acceptance of each other and an appreciation of our individuality. Help me to appreciate the specialness of each person.

Daily Prayer # 39

"Surely goodness and love will follow me all the days of my life, and I will dwell in the house of the Lord forever."
Psalm 23: 6

Lord – My spirit is willing to be excellent in all I do, but sometimes the flesh is weak. There is a weariness that tries to come over me and look for a short cut or easier path. These are the times I need You the most. Please recharge my batteries today. Give me an encouraging word to keep putting one foot in front of the other knowing that I am right where You want me and that the final outcome today, next week, next month, and a year from now is in Your hands.

Daily Prayer # 40

"My son – my daughter – pay attention to what I say; listen closely to my words. Do not let them out of your sight, keep them within your heart; for they are life to those who find them and health to a man's whole body. Above all else, guard your heart, for it is the wellspring of life." Proverbs 4: 20 – 23

Lord – I want the words of my mouth to stop contradicting the faith and word in my heart. I keep cancelling my proclamation of Your promises with my negative statements. Renew my thinking – then renew my mouth to align with Your Word. Thank you that every day is a new day and all my negative words of doubt and unbelief are under washed in the blood of Jesus. Let my mouth be the compass for my life and direct me to You and Your blessings.

 Workplace Wisdom

On the Tarmac

At the San Francisco airport, just before sunrise, I sat on the tarmac (runway) for 40 minutes waiting for a thunder storm to pass. We were #1 for takeoff when the storm suddenly passed through.

I could see the lights on the runway out the window I wondered if I would make my connection in Dallas. I began writing in my journal some thoughts I had about my vision to build a leadership center and I heard the inner voice of the Lord say, "You're on the tarmac Wendy."

I realized that I was very close to take off for what God had been preparing me for the past 25 years. To what God has always referred to as my "747" ministry.

I realized that when it was time, God would give the signal (from the tower) and the ministry would take off not one minute sooner and safe from any danger of a pending storm.

Even though I can see the end of the runway – I certainly cannot see the final destination. I don't even have access to the flight plan.

Type "A" personalities – high achievers – don't like tarmac experiences. Yet – because of the pause at the runway – I was able to hear the voice of the Lord. Out the window, after the storm passed, a rainbow appeared sending God's love and assurance that everything will come to pass on its appointed day.

Daily Prayer # 41

"For if you possess these qualities (faith, goodness, knowledge, self-control, perseverance, godliness, brotherly kindness, and love), in increasing measure, they will keep you from being ineffective and unproductive..."
2 Peter 1: 8

Lord –If a vision for my life is delayed because I am not mature enough to handle it – then grow me up. If You are worried that success will go to my head – then give me a spirit of humility. If You are concerned that I can't handle finances then give me a spirit of discipline and generosity. If You think that I will become short tempered under pressure – then give me a spirit of love and self-control. I can do all things through Christ who strengthens me.

Daily Prayer # 42

"By wisdom the Lord laid the earth's foundations, by understanding He set the heavens in place; by His knowledge the deeps were divided, and the clouds let drop the dew." Proverbs 3: 19

Lord – I often worry that my education and experiences will not be enough to be all You want me to be. Then I remember that all the learning in the world does not compare to the presence of God. Even Moses gave up His Egyptian title to follow You. Let Your life in me be enough to lead others and let the wisdom of Moses be upon me today to lead people to the promise land of faith.

Daily Prayer # 43

"In the same way, let your light shine before men, that they may see your good deeds and praise your Father in heaven." Matthew 5: 6

Lord – I want to be a God pleaser – not a people pleaser. If everything I did was to bring more of You in my life rather than more people into my camp – then I would experience your peace and joy whether people liked me or not. Show me how to lift You up in the presence of others without teaching or preaching. Show me how to have Your light and presence so bright and powerful that people will be drawn to Your Saving Grace. Equip me to do that.

Daily Prayer # 44

"Come to me, all you who are weary and burdened, and I will give you rest." Matthew 11: 28

Lord – I know there were times that David, Moses, Job, Apostle Paul, and even Jesus were weary. But they always looked to You in those times and drew their strength from being in Your presence. Help me to find a quiet time today where You and I can have communion. In that time, I pray that I will be renewed. Make me energetic, full of joy, and strong enough to face any challenge. Thank you for lifting my spirits and strengthening my body. Cause me to be grateful for the good things You do in my life and don't let the enemy of discontentment, discouragement, or fear take hold in any way. I resist the enemy of my thoughts and heart in Jesus' name.

Daily Prayer # 45

"Our Father in heaven, hallowed be Your name, Your kingdom come, Your will be done on earth as it is in heaven." Matthew 5: 9

Lord – I think we are going into a kingdom age - a time when the Kingdom of Heaven is demonstrated on earth in a greater way. I think there is coming a season when multitudes are going to come to the church and receive the "manna" (bread) from heaven once again. I believe that a great hunger for God will be in people's lives and the first people they approach will be their friends and neighbors who stood strong morally and emotionally under pressure. Prepare me to be used as circumstances cause people to search for answers. Prepare me to have answers to their tough questions. Keep me refreshed so that I may be a refreshing in their lives.

Daily Prayer # 46

"Blessed are the peacemakers, for they will be called sons of God." Matthew 5: 9

Lord – Conflict is normal. As much as I want peace on earth – it does not exist as long as there are people who disagree. Personality differences are understandable but irritability and coarseness disrupts the peace. You call it "living in the flesh" and where flesh rules there is chaos. I pray that the fruit of gentleness and kindness through me can bring order in the chaos. I ask that my prayers make a difference. I proclaim your peace and love in this place today.

Daily Prayer # 47

"Yet I hold this against you: You have forsaken your first love." Revelation 2: 4

Lord – I know you want us to not forget the "first love" experience we had when we found You. But the circumstances of life and the ugliness of the sin in the world keeps a thick fog over us and You seem so much further away than when we first believed. Help me to understand that You live in my heart and that You are with me always. Teach me what that means and help me to hear You and experience You fresh each day. Let me feel your presence even in the chaos and noise of the day. I don't just want to know it in my head – I want to experience it every day in my heart like the day we first met.

Daily Prayer # 48

"Why do you look at the speck of sawdust tin your brother's eye and pay no attention to the plank in your own eye?" Matthew 7: 3

Lord – Remove my critical eye. Help me not to see the faults of others – but rather keep my eye on my own heart condition. We are all called to be leaders for You. As a leader, give me a desire to coach, train, and develop the skills of others. Thank you for those who were patient with me and invested in my development. Give me a teacher's heart and develop my skills with the fruits of the Spirit. As I grow and mature in my own journey – help me to share wisdom You have taught me with others.

Daily Prayer # 49

"For the revelation awaits the appointed time; it speaks of the end and will not prove false. Though it linger, wait for it; it will certainly come and will not delay." Habakkuk 2: 3

Lord –All Christians are waiting for some form of breakthrough - breakthrough in a marriage, in a job, in finding a spouse or in the salvation of loved ones. No matter how much we believe or run in the right direction – we just don't get there. Then suddenly, when we think we will never get into the promise land – breakthrough. If this is a spiritual "muscle-building-fitness-plan" designed by You, then help me to accept your strategy, help me to keep on praying and believing, and help me to finish the race.

Daily Prayer # 50

"Be diligent in these matters; give yourself wholly to them, so that everyone may see your progress." 1 Timothy 4: 15

Lord – People who have great success don't waste time. Help me to be productive with every precious moment that You give me. Keep me from temptation to want to throw in the towel, give up, or be lazy. Pace my footsteps so that I complete everything within the right time and with just the right amount of energy so that I don't grow weary. Help me to live a healthy life style that I may live long, enjoy all the days of my life, and show forth the joy of Your salvation for many years to come.

✍ Workplace Wisdom

My Dog ZuZu

We had a dog named ZuZu who went to pet Heaven in 2010 at age 7-years. At age 5-years, he went completely blind. We didn't let him in the backyard in California unless we were home because of the swimming pool.

In the beginning, he fell in a few times. We had pool-trained all our dogs – taking them in the water and showing them where the steps are located. ZuZu remembered his training.

When ZuZu fell in, he knew that the steps were there – but not sure where. He would calmly follow the edge of the pool, paddling until his feet hit the steps. Sometimes I would jump in to rescue him – but usually he was on his way out of the water by the time I reached him.

This was an amazing feat for this breed of dog – short of a miracle – because Chinese Shar-peis typically can't swim. Their heads are too big and their feet to small – so they eventually sink. God gave ZuZu big feet – so he was equipped to survive. I think we can take a lesson from ZuZu.

If he had panicked and tried to pull his wet body out of the edge of the pool where he fell in – he would have become exhausted and given up. Instead, he stayed calm and by "faith" and memory of the promise that there were steps, he kept going forward.

After a couple times of success – learning that the steps would indeed always be there – he found his way more quickly to the path of safety.

Even if we are barely treading water – if we move toward our goal, we will eventually reach it. If we stay calm and focused – keeping our spiritual eyes fixed on God's promises – we will find our way out of every situation. If we panic – we may miss the path to success.

Yes, God will come to the rescue – but in the end – He wants us to learn to trust what He has promised and keep putting one foot in front of the other.

It did not give me joy to see ZuZu suffer with his blindness, but it does give me joy to see how carefully God cared for him and I can trust He will care for me.

Have there been times in your career where you feel you were swimming blind and not sure where you were headed? How did it turn out? Recalling what God did for us in the past gives us assurance for our future.

Meditate or write down the times God rescued you and everything turned out just fine. If you are waiting for breakthrough in your job, career or vision – what actions can you take to not panic and keep swimming?

Daily Prayer # 51

"Consider it pure joy, my brothers [and sisters], whenever you face trials of many kinds, because you know that the testing of your faith develops perseverance." James 1: 3

Lord – We would not know pleasure without knowing pain. We would not know Your Power without trials in our life. We would not know that You answer prayers if circumstances did not drive us to pray. Help me to receive test and trials not as an opportunity to be fearful and discouraged, but as an opportunity to know You and Your power. Let me become more Christ-like in the fire of correction and purification. Help me to keep my eyes on Jesus and to know that there is light at the end of the tunnel and pleasure in the promise land.

Daily Prayer # 52

"You are awesome, O God, in your sanctuary; the God of Israel gives power and strength to his people. Praise be to God!" Psalms 68: 35

Lord – There is a song in my heart – "Bless the Lord, oh my soul, and all that is within me – bless His Holy Name." I believe in You Lord. I thought You might like to hear that today. In a world that acts as if You don't exist. I want to encourage Your heart today and tell you that I believe in Your Son. I believe He lives in my heart. I believe in Your Holy Spirit that guides and teaches me. I believe You are the Creator of the universe. What else do we need on this earth if we have You? I believe you are with me today.

Daily Prayer # 53

"Whatever you do, work at it with all your heart, as working for the Lord, not for men, since you know that you will receive an inheritance from the Lord as a reward. It is the Lord Christ you are serving." Colossians 3: 23 – 24

Lord – Help me to remember that work is of You. Paul worked as a tent maker as he ministered. He didn't complain that he had to work to make a living. In fact, he told the Christian workers to "get a job!" If you intend for us to work, then you will provide the work. Work ethic is important to You, whether we labor for a harvest of souls, labor for a harvest in the field, labor at companies, or labor in our homes. Give me acceptance with joy for the opportunity to work.

Daily Prayer # 54

"He was oppressed and afflicted, yet He did not open his mouth; He was led like lamb to the slaughter, and as a sheep before her shearers is silent, so He did not open His mouth." Isaiah 53: 7

Lord – We call the day that Jesus was crucified, "Good Friday." What seemed like a terrible evil, was actually a redemptive plan for all mankind. You were silent when Jesus hung on the cross and it appeared as if all was lost and abandoned. In actuality, victory was just around the corner. Help me to know that in the silent times, breakthrough is just around the corner. When I don't hear Your voice, let Your scriptures bring me hope. Give me the assurance that you are in control.

Daily Prayer # 55

"So Shadrach, Meshach and Abednego came out of the fire...They saw that the fire had not harmed their bodies, nor was a hair of their heads singed; their robes were not scorched, and there was no smell of fire on them." Daniel 3: 26b – 27

Lord – I can feel the loss of others – loss of job, loss of home, loss of loved ones, loss of health, or loss of finances. The enemy would tell people that this loss of resources means that they have lost Your love. Help people to remember that Jesus said He could not remove us from the world, but to not fear because He had overcome the world. We have the power to get through to the other side. Give us hope today that we will come out of the fire without the smell of smoke on us.

Daily Prayer # 56

"God is our refuge and strength, an ever present help in trouble. Therefore we will not fear, though the earth give way and the mountains fall into the heart of the sea . . ." Psalms 46: 1

Lord – I am tired of the news reports. I am tired of the foolishness of man's wisdom. I look to You for truth. I look to You for my future. I do not fear war, epidemics, flood, or fire. I only fear You and I want to follow You all the days of my life. I look to Your word for answers and I refuse to compromise. You are my refuge and strength and I will depend on You. I will fear no evil, for You are with me (Psalm 23).

Daily Prayer # 57

"Before I formed you in the womb I knew you, before you were born I set you apart; I appointed you as a prophet to the nations." Jeremiah 1: 5

Lord – Every once in a while a negative experience from my past occupies my thoughts and feelings. A sin, a mistake, or regret tries to convict me. The enemy wants me to walk in guilt and condemnation, but You want me to walk in freedom and forgiveness. Help me to accept that You knew me BEFORE I was in my mother's womb and that everything that happened to me was all part of a plan. Turn everything into good and help me to silence the enemy's voice in my head through Your Name.

Daily Prayer # 58

"For he will command his angels concerning you to guard you in all your ways; they will lift you up in their hands, so that you will not strike your foot against a stone." Psalms 91: 11 – 12

Lord – I need to see and know that the activities of my day give You glory. Your Word indicates that giving all of our God-given gifts to the world with all our heart is a form of worship to You. I pray that my excellence in all my tasks honors You. Increase those moments that I can pass Your love and wisdom on to others. I pray the angels will give me Divine encounters. I pray that You will express Your love to me in those little ways that tell me You are with me and that your angels are on assignment on my behalf.

Daily Prayer # 59

"Blessed is the man who perseveres under trial, because when he has stood the test, he will receive the crown of life that God has promised to those who love Him." James 1: 12

Lord – A vision is a wonderful thing and imagination is a gift from you. It is waiting for the vision to come to pass that builds character. Help me to trust that you are working in my life during my waiting season. When I want to give up the dream, please inspire me again. Reveal to me anything I need to do in my time of wait so that I am prepared for the suddenly that is on its way.

Daily Prayer # 60

"That which was from the beginning, which we have heard, which we have seen with our eyes, which we have looked at and our hands have touched – this we proclaim concerning the Word of life." I John 1: 1

Lord – People today debate if the Bible is truly the Word of God. I am not a scholar – but I know that Your Word has strengthen me, healed me, delivered me, and enlightened me. I am not the same because of Your Word. It is full of life, light, and power. It is full of You and I want more of You in my life. Today and every day I supernaturally receive Your Word in my spirit, soul, and body.

✎ Workplace Wisdom

Run With Horses

"If you have run with footmen, and they have wearied you, then how can you contend with horses? And if in the land of peace, in which you trusted, they wearied you, then how will you do in the floodplain of the Jordan?" (Jeremiah 12:5).

Jeremiah, an Old Testament prophet, was given the task of warning the people to get their act right with God. After a few attempts with no success, he complained to God about the people. God responded: with the message about horses.

What God is saying is if we can't pass the test with small challenges and personality conflicts, we are not ready for greater leadership responsibility. The same is true in our service to the Lord.

If we are not being faithful in the little things or managing the level of finances He has given us, then we are not ready for the increase or the bigger vision.

God has chosen us for an assignment, but in order to qualify us, He puts us in situations to prepare us for what He wants us to do. Our spiritual growth and our physical responsibilities with work, family, community and church are very integrated.

God's ultimate goal for us is to "run and not be weary" and to bear the fruits of the spirit in the face of a complaining generation. The higher up on the management ladder you go, the more personalities and differences of opinion you will experience.

Give each day and each situation to the Lord and allow each situation become a new step of strength in your life. Soon you'll be riding on the horses and across the floodplains, and it will seem easy because the Lord has groomed you for the task.

Using your strengths will make you more motivated in your job and increase energy and productivity. Don't know your strengths? Go to **www.strengthsfinder.com**. I consider this an important step in discovering the gifts and talents God gave you – it's worth the investment of the small fee to take the test. Leverage off of your strengths in each situation and delegate out assignments that are not your strengths.

Daily Prayer # 61

"Let your eyes look straight ahead, fix your gaze directly before you. Make level paths for your feet and take only ways that are firm. Do not swerve to the right of the left; keep your foot from evil." Proverbs 4: 25 – 27

Lord – Your Word is clear that we must move forward and follow a plan. Forgive me for moving off paths to the right or to the left. Help me to look to You and look to the goals you have set before me. Keep me from wavering and make me sure footed. Help me to climb mountains for you. I pray for your peace and strength to not consider the journey that I just completed but rather to trust with faith and joy the next stage of my life that You have planned.

Daily Prayer # 62

"Enlarge the place of your tent, stretch your tent curtains wide, do not hold back; lengthen your cords, strengthen your stakes, for you will spread out to the right and to the left . . ." Isaiah 54: 2 - 3a

Lord – It is my tendency to stay close to shore or stay safe in the boat. Yet, you wanted Peter to step out in faith and walk on water. Unless I step out in faith and launch the "ship of my destiny," I will not know the great things you can do for me. Help me to not hold on to the natural and give me the courage to dive into the supernatural. Help me to not consider if I am going to sink, float, or swim. Help me to depend completely on You and keep my eyes fixed on Jesus.

Daily Prayer # 63

". . . no weapon forged against you will prevail . . ."
Isaiah 54:17

Lord – As a swimmer, I know that if I am calm, relaxed, and lay on my back, I will float. Resting in You creates more strength than a dog paddle that goes nowhere. Help me to have peace and calm when I am way out in the deep Cause me to receive guidance from You and not from others. This is a season where I have to completely trust You. Help me to cling to nothing but Jesus. Give me a sense today that You have EVERYTHING in your control and that no weapon formed against me by the enemy will prosper.

Daily Prayer # 64

"He who dwells in the shelter of the Most High will rest in
the shadow of the Almighty. I will say of the Lord, 'He is
my refuge and my fortress, my God, in whom I trust.'"
Psalm 91: 1 – 2

Lord – Help me to not jump ahead of you to make the plan for my life come to pass in my time. I need You to do the moving in the right direction and in the right time. Satan's biggest trick is to distract me and pull me out of my rest in You. I know from experience that all great things of God happen in REST not in anxious works. Don't let the enemy pull me out of Your rest today and keep me in Your love and blessing. I trust you with my life.

Daily Prayer # 65

"I tell you the truth, if you have faith as small as a mustard seed, you can say to this mountain, 'Move from here to there' and it will move. Nothing will be impossible for you.'Matthew 17: 20

Lord – A pastor once said that we all have a fulltime 3-fold ministry: Loving people, doing good and kicking the hell out of the devil! I am reminded to not only show justice, mercy, love, and goodness in the workplace – but to also do spiritual warfare. Bless the sword of my prayers to destroy the strongholds that try to destroy God's will from being done in my life, in my family, in my church, and in my nation.

Daily Prayer # 66

"Now Abel kept flocks and Cain worked the soil. In the course of time Cain brought some of the fruits of the soil as an offering to the Lord. But Abel brought fat portions from some of the firstborn of his flock. The Lord looked with favor on Abel and his offering." Genesis 4: 2 – 4

Lord – Cain tried to give You the product (grain) of his own works rather than the sacrifice of obedience to what You required. I am reminded that none of my works make me right with You. You love and accept me because of the sacrifice of Jesus Christ. Holy Spirit, help me to seek the Lord early in the morning – the first moments of the day - to draw my strength from Him and to be reminded that it is through Him and through resting in Him alone that I can do all things.

Daily Prayer # 67

"Noah did everything just as God commanded him."
Genesis 6: 22

Lord – The Bible says that Noah walked in habitual fellowship with God and found favor in the eyes of the Lord (6: 8 - 9). Wow! How can I do that? There must be only one way – talk to You more often, listen to Your direction, read Your Word, reach out to others with love, pray for others, and rest in Your peace and love. If I want more of You in my life – there are actions that I need to take. When challenges come, I want an ark like Noah's not just a little life raft. I desire Your favor in my life. Fellowship with You is *my* responsibility.

Daily Prayer # 68

"Who of you by worrying can add a single hour to his [or her] life." Matthew 6:27

Lord – Time is so precious. Why do we waste them with worry when you are on the throne of our lives? Help me to reserve my energy to accomplish the tasks I have today. Take care of my finances and heal any broken relationships. I rebuke the voices of worry in my head that are trying to get into my heart and shake my faith in You. I will not bow down to worry but rather lift my voice in praise and thanksgiving to the Lord of my life.

Daily Prayer # 69

"Then He told them many things in parables, saying: 'A farmer went out to sow the seed. . . It fell among thorns, which grew up and choked the plants." Matthew 13: 3

Lord – It is hard to produce more grapes – more fruit – in a vineyard that has weeds and thorns. The weeds are constantly trying to choke me out. At times it seems that a lot of effort produces a very small crop. Please come into my garden and tend it. Remove the obstacles and rocks. Put out the fires and remove the nettles of the enemy. As I abide in You, You promised to abide in me. Help me bloom in my garden. Help me to succeed in the tasks set before me.

Daily Prayer # 70

"We have different gifts according to the grace given us." Romans 12:6

Lord – Your gifts are not just for Christians to give to other Christians. Your gifts are for anyone You are trying to reach with Your love. A prophetic gift could bring a message to an unbeliever. The gift of encouragement could minister to someone near me. The gift of wisdom can operate at a meeting not just a Bible study. The gift of teacher can mean coaching someone in sports or education. The world does not recognize You – but perhaps it will recognize Your love, wisdom, peace, and power through the gifts that You give us to give to them. Let a portion of the gifts you have given me flow to others today.

✍ Workplace Wisdom

The Same Wind

One night I asked my husband, "Why does the favor on my jobs keep changing?" I did not have favor at my last job – in fact, I was persecuted, kept from using my talents, and made some regrettable mistakes. I worked hard for business sales and I prayed for blessing on the programs that I ran – but the success was minimal. In my current job, I applied the same marketing and sales principles (and prayers) and I had extreme favor and success for three years. Currently, sales are down and I struggle once again with favor.

I asked again, "I have not changed in my walk with God – what makes the difference?" He replied that he didn't know.

Then we turned on the television and listened to a preacher. He shared how he was jogging one day and a wind came up against him. It was so strong, he could hardly run and it was exhausting.

He did not think he could do one more lap and was about to quit. Suddenly, the wind shifted and was at his back. It was pushing him along and he completed to the finish line. He said, "The wind of adversity in your life will become the same wind that carries you to the finish line, if you persevere and trust God."

My husband turned to me and said, "There's your answer. Your last job actually prepared you for this job. In fact, you would not have this job if you had not worked at your former job and you would not have been prepared for the pressures of this job. Perhaps what you are going through now is preparing your for something greater in the future."

He continued, "You also would not have the knowledge you have that you share with other leaders. You would not be ministering to others through Marketplace Christians without the trials and the struggles. God's ways always have a higher purpose."

I realized that God's favor was upon me in both situations – when there was prosperity and when there seemed to be lack. When we are seeking Him and obeying Him, His glory and purpose in all things will be revealed. Even adversity can be His favor in our lives, but it takes maturity and wisdom to see it.

Are there circumstances related to your job that don't seem fair and just? Does it seem like people who work less get more reward – or at the least, get away with it?

Share your concerns with God in prayer. Is there some character qualities being built in your life as a result of these circumstances? Evaluate who you are today and compare it to a year ago. Celebrate your growth in the Lord and write down what He has done in your life.

Daily Prayer # 71

"Humble yourselves, therefore, under God's mighty hand, that He may lift you up in due time. Cast all your anxiety on Him because He cares for you." 1 Peter 5: 6 – 7

Lord – The season of pruning is not easy. I know there is a time to cut old things away and make room for the new. The pruning season feels like winter and how I long for spring. You knew we would have anxiety in these times because You told us to cast it on You. Thank you for reminding me that You care for me in the pruning season and that it is in this time that my roots will go down deep to prepare for the new growth. This is not the end – it is the beginning of a great and awesome plan.

Daily Prayer # 72

"Dear children, let us not love with words or tongue but with actions and in truth." I John 3: 19

Lord – You alone are the developer of souls. You use Your people around us and the circumstances they create to bring us closer to You. Even though I have had major trials over the years with co-workers and bosses - I trust that You are Lord of all circumstances. Help me to speak truth when required, to show love when needed, and to leave the final conclusion in Your hands. Remind me that I am only one stepping stone of guidance in someone else's journey. I will not know the results of many of my actions until that eternal report card.

Daily Prayer # 73

"Blessed are the pure in heart for they shall see God."
Matthew 5: 8

Lord – The laws of self-defense in Karate are: 1) Have a clean heart; 2) Maintain a steadfast spirit; and 3) Follow your purpose. How interesting that walking in these three things brings power and protection. Similarly, Your word says: 1) Depart from sin and keep a pure heart; 2) Stay faithful to God's Word; and 3) Obey God and follow His plan for your life. Cleanse my heart from any selfishness or worldly desires. Keep me on a straight path. Cause me to have a pure heart and to always obey You. Guide and protect me from the evil one until that day I meet You face-to-face and hear You say "Well done my good and faithful servant."

Daily Prayer # 74

"For the eyes of the Lord range throughout the earth to strengthen those whose hearts are fully committed to Him." II Chronicles 16: 9

Lord – The Amplified Bible version of this verse says that You want to "show Yourself strong on my behalf." I am humbled by such a concept. Defend me in the midst of my enemies. Do not let them rule over me. Give me victory. Let Your favor and mercy be upon me. Give me favor with my responsibilities, my calling, my tasks, my workload, my time, and my resources. Whatever lies ahead – show Yourself strong on my behalf. I need You each and every day.

Daily Prayer # 75

"Their descendants will be known among the nations and their offspring among the people. All who see them will acknowledge that they are a people the Lord has blessed." Isaiah 61: 9

Lord – Moses asked for Your favor and blessing so that the world and Your enemies would know that you are with Your people. We need Your favor in hard economic times so that the world will know You take care of those whose hearts are after You. It is not a boastful or prideful attitude – I simply believe Your Word. Help me to not be pulled into the fear and anxiety of the world and to keep my heart receptive to Your blessing in faith.

Daily Prayer # 76

"Then I heard the voice of the Lord saying, 'Whom shall I send? And who will go for us?" And I said, 'Here am I. Send me!' He said, 'Go and tell this people: Be ever hearing, but never understanding; be ever seeing, but never perceiving.'" Isaiah 6: 8 – 9

Lord – It is hard to go to a hard-hearted and blind generation of people in a nation where people have everything and think they don't need God. Prepare the way and soften hearts so that when I speak Your truth and love – they will receive. Don't let my words fall to the ground unfruitful. Purify my lips and bless the words of my mouth. Raise up intercessors – prayer warriors – to stand in the gap for this lost generation. Let my prayers make a difference in this nation.

Daily Prayer # 77

"...for the gracious hand of his God was on him. For Ezra had devoted himself to the study and observance of the Law of the Lord, and to teaching its decrees and laws in Israel." Ezra 7: 8 – 10

Lord – Your gracious hand will be upon me when I study Your word. You can use mightily one whose whole heart craves a knowledge of You. Your hand is upon those who seek You. It's hard to imagine how awesome it is to have the hand of God – the God of the universe – upon me. I am humbled by the thought of your presence in my life. Let Your hand be upon Your saints to do great and mighty things for You.

Daily Prayer # 78

"In your hearts set apart Christ as Lord. Always be prepared to give an answer to everyone who asks you to give the reason for the hope that you have. But do this with gentleness and respect, keeping a clear conscience, so that those who speak maliciously against your good behavior in Christ may be ashamed of their slander." I Peter 3:15 – 16

Lord – Grow me in my ability to give a logical defense of my faith. I want to give my reason for hope to anyone who asks and I pray that you will bless my simple message. Help me to explain Your love and your grace courageously and respectfully. Even in the face of a defensive or argumentative person – show me how to gently give a right answer. I pray that You will always give me the right words in the hour that I need them.

Daily Prayer # 79

"So Pharaoh said to Joseph,' I hereby put you in charge of the whole land of Egypt.'" Genesis 41: 41

Lord – Joseph is such a wonderful example of how You prepare a leader. He was told in a dream of His greatness – but his journey was through slavery, loneliness, rejection, lowliness, false accusations, and persecution. For thirteen years he was in slavery, yet he learned to forgive, manage people, resist temptation, speak the truth, oversee resources, and share vision and wisdom. Help me to trust You in my journey and make me a Joseph in my assignments.

Daily Prayer # 80

"The Lord has blessed my master abundantly, and he has become wealthy." Genesis 24: 35

Lord – I proclaim your promises: "God will supply all my need," "God owns all the resources I need," "God is the source of my ideas and creativity," God will rebuke the devourer on my behalf," "God will bring the mountain down," "God is on time – He is never late," "God will bless the work of my hands," and "I am under the blessing and not the curse." May Your words establish me today.

 Workplace Wisdom

Pressing On – Pressing In

"We are hard-pressed on every side, yet not crushed; we are perplexed, but not in despair; persecuted, but not forsaken; struck down, but not destroyed" (2 Corinthians 4: 6-7).

There are certain times in history when one generation believes they dealt with more pressure than the previous generation. Survivors of the Great Depression or World War II, think the current generation is extremely blessed.

The truth is that Christians today have their own level of pressure and anxiety. We deal with new technology, workplace pressures, single parenting, inflation, high mortgages and low paying jobs, to name a few.

Apostle Paul wrote a great deal about how to endure the pressures of the world, and he reminds us that even in difficult times we can always sense God's sustainability in our lives.

Paul explains why we have these pressures: "For we who live are always being delivered to death for Jesus' sake, that the life of Jesus may be manifested in our mortal flesh" (2 Corinthians 4:11). As one Texas pastor put it: "As the outward body suffers and deteriorates the inward man accelerates in growth."

The pressure in our lives releases God's glory for others to see. When Paul pleaded with the Lord to make Satan stop tormenting him, the Lord said: "My grace is sufficient for you, for my strength is made perfect in weakness" (2 Corinthians 12: 9). Paul told the Christ followers, "I take pleasure in infirmities, in reproaches, in needs, in persecutions, in distresses, for Christ's sake. For when I am weak, then I am strong" (V. 10). We have to remember that it is not always about us – it's about God's glory *in* us.

So what are we to do? We are to *press on* and *press in*. We press on to finish the task God has called us, to pursue the dream we have in our heart, and to run the race to the finish line – to be made in His likeness as we cross over into heaven. To receive strength, we are to press in to Jesus, and He will give us the ability and grace to endure as we run the race.

Endurance in the race comes from practice. When athletes prepare for a race, in the beginning they are short of breath and have cramps in their legs. If they continue to practice on a daily basis, their endurance builds and it gets easier. Through pressing on with life and pressing in to Jesus each and every day, we will have the strength of God within us and be ready to endure successfully any future pressures.

Leader John Maxwell wrote about Apostle Paul's thorn in the flesh: "Instead of getting angry at his thorn (weakness) and the way it slowed him down, Paul relished how weak it made him. Why? It kept him in close dependence on the power of God. Paul understood that the weaker he was, the stronger God became within him. When there is less of you as a leader, there is more of God as the Leader."

Daily Prayer # 81

"Dear friend, I pray that you may enjoy good health and that all may go well with you, even as your soul is getting along well <prospering>." 3 John 2-4

Lord – My spirit must prosper if I am to prosper. Living in Your Word brings increase. The battle is in my faith – not in my pocket book. If I seek You first – everything else will be taken care of (Matthew 6:33). If I expose my mind to Christ Jesus – which is the Word of God – I will grow in leaps and bounds. Do not let me depart from this plan of action that you require of us.

Daily Prayer # 82

"Joseph named his firstborn Manasseh and said, 'It is because God has made me forget all my trouble and all my father's household.' The second son he named Ephraim and said, 'It is because God has made me fruitful in the land of my suffering.'" Genesis 41: 51 & 52

Lord – My country is not everything I want it to be right now. It is a harsh place for a Christian to live. Thank you for Your promise that like Joseph – I can be fruitful in the land of oppression. The worldview cannot dictate my peace, joy or blessing in You. Your love for me, Your provision for me, and your peace for me is not dictated by the world's circumstances. I choose to keep my eyes on You today.

Daily Prayer # 83

"They will soar on wings like eagles; they will run and not grow weary, they will walk and not be faint." Isaiah 40: 31

Lord – Let the winds of adversity carry me to new heights with You. Allow the winds to carry me as the eagle. When I experience opposition, stress, crisis, or constant change, help me to stop, face the circumstances and let you lift my spirit in the midst of these events. Thank you for being the wind beneath my wings.

Daily Prayer # 84

"Solomon also had twelve district governors over all Israel, who supplied provisions for the king and the royal household." I Kings 4: 7

Lord – Solomon had the kind of leadership and dominion over the land that God wants us to have. There was nothing lacking and he led with excellence. When I imagine that he had 12 officers to take care of all the details – including feeding 40,000 horses (verse 28) – I know nothing is impossible with God. You will provide all the resources to lead in the calling You have for me. Open my mind and heart to receive every resource I need to achieve Your goals.

Daily Prayer # 85

"So give your servant a discerning heart to govern your people and to distinguish between right and wrong. For who is able to govern this great people of yours?" (Solomon) I Kings 3: 9

Lord – Leadership and governorship has always been part of Your plan. Your people need good rulers and the best rulers ask You for wisdom. Help me to also have a wise answer for everything that comes before me. Let me know what to say and teach me what to do in all situations. Oh that all Your people would understand and believe that your arm is not too short for our limitations, our families, our government, and our nation.

Daily Prayer # 86

"No one from the east or the west or from the desert can exalt a man. But it is God who judges: He brings one down, he exalts another." Psalm 75: 6 – 7

Lord – Promotions come from You. Release comes from You. Deliverance comes from You. Help me to keep You as my first priority making decisions in accordance with Your word. I trust You with my life. You alone know the path set before me and the hearts of those in authority over me are in Your hands. I will not fear what man can do to me. You are my Lord and where one door closes another will open because goodness and mercy will follow me all the days of my life (Psalm 23).

Daily Prayer # 87

"There is a time for everything, and a season for every activity under heaven . . ." Ecclesiastes 3: 1

Lord – When I look at the fall colors I am amazed at how you provide seasons for our pleasure. You knew we needed change and color in our life. The refreshment on the first cool fall day takes away the sting of the summer heat. How marvelous that the process of trees "dying" is a beautiful celebration of colors as if to say, "The last season was wonderful but now it is time to prepare for an even greater season ahead." As You prune off the old to prepare for the new, let me celebrate with joy and expectation the good things You are about to perform.

Daily Prayer # 88

"I looked for a man among them who would build up the wall and stand before me in the gap on behalf of the land so I would not have to destroy it, but I found none." Ezekiel 22: 30

Lord – You have shown me in my heart that the "gap" is people and nations not connected to God. Do You mean I can be that link on their behalf? Do You mean that my prayers can help prevent disaster from coming upon this nation? If yes – then I am not doing my job. I need to pray more for the people to soften their hearts toward God so that Your blessing can come forth. Remind me to stand in the gap for the leaders of this nation and those in authority.

Daily Prayer # 89

"Create in me a pure heart, O God, and renew a steadfast spirit within me. Do not cast me from your presence or take your Holy Spirit form me. Restore to me the joy of your salvation and grant me a willing spirit, to sustain me." Psalm 51: 10 - 12

Lord – Help me to remember that winter seasons make the beauty of spring all the more wonderful. There is always a next season. There is always a next stage in our lives. There is always a bend in the road and something just around the corner. Do not let me get content in the quiet time or calm season. Do not let me forget the vision. Renew a right heart within me and stir the vision once again.

Daily Prayer # 90

"A time to rend and a time to sew, a time to keep silence and a time to speak. . ." Ecclesiastes 3:7

Lord – In the military the orders are sometimes sealed until it is the appropriate time to reveal the next steps. You don't always reveal everything right away. Sealed orders are for our own protection. Satan cannot read sealed orders. You have a bigger plan that we don't quite see. Help me to trust that the orders for my life are in Your hands – in safe keeping and that the appointed time will come.

 Workplace Wisdom

Cowboy Wisdom

"I know that nothing is better for them than to rejoice and to do good in their lives, and also that every man should eat and drink and enjoy the good of all his labor – it is the gift of God" (Ecclesiastes: 3: 12 – 13).

In our Texas home I had pictures of horses and cowboys. In one painting, the cattle are not walking, but rather grazing in the pasture, as the cowboy sits on his horse overseeing and protecting.

With my personality style, I would rather have the cattle running with my horse going at a nice trot next to them. The Lord was trying to give me a message that "not stampeding" can be a good thing.

I researched cowboys and found that cattle drives had to strike a balance between speed and the weight of the cattle. While cattle could be driven 25 miles a day, they would lose so much weight they couldn't be sold at the end of the trail.

By going shorter distances each day, the cattle were allowed to rest and graze twice a day. Maintaining a slow pace meant that it took two months to travel from a ranch to a railroad station, as some trails were 1,000 miles long.

Perhaps if we had a clear understanding of why the Lord has us travel at a slower pace at times, we could better endure the wait for the suddenly we are hoping will come. Here are a few good reasons why the Lord wants us to pace our lives:

1. If we go too fast, we could miss a new course of direction that He is trying to steer us toward (no pun intended).
2. If we don't pace ourselves, we may not want to stop on the trail to minister to someone the Lord brings in our path. (We'll use the excuse we are in a hurry).
3. If we don't schedule stopping points, we will be worn out at the end of the trail.
4. Feeding on the Word of the Lord along the way for nourishment and direction is what the Lord intends.
5. Slowness in one area of our life allows us to spend time in another area that we normally are too busy to attend to. (I learned that the cowboys wrote lots of songs and poetry!)
6. We need to enjoy the fruit of our labor – not just focus on the labor.
7. We need to be obedient because the Lord is also watching out for our safety and He knows best what lies ahead.

Going with the flow and pacing ourselves is actually a "change skill" that corporations are looking for in employees. It's called "flexibility." There is definitely an ebb and flow in organizations that produce products or delivers services.

Instead of stressing and complaining about these situations, we need to see a pattern and begin to go with it.

Daily Prayer # 91

"A time to weep and a time to laugh. . ." Ecclesiastes 3: 4

Lord – Mourning over the loss of a pet, friend, loved one, home, job, or spouse is hard on the soul and the flesh. We want to be cheerful but the joy is not there. How did David move forward so quickly after the loss of his baby? The joy of the Lord must have been his strength. Help me to draw more from Your joy and the knowledge that joy comes in the morning. I place all my sadness over any loss into your hands. As I do, I see the holes in Your hands and I am reminded that you suffered for our pain. Thank you Jesus. I look forward to that time of laughter.

Daily Prayer # 92

"Love is patient, love is kind. It does not envy, it does not boast, it is not proud. It is not rude, it is not self-seeking, it is not easily angered, it keeps no record of wrongs." I Corinthians 13: 4 – 5

Lord – Wow! If this is our measuring stick for love, I am not hitting the mark. It's hard to endure poor customer service, rude drivers, unkind people, late planes, and heavy workloads. It's easy to be irritable and touchy in challenging situations. I want to reflect Your love and patience so I am going to need more of You. Fill me up so that I hardly notice when others do wrong and keep me from doing wrong to others.

Daily Prayer # 93

"Do not be overcome by evil, but overcome evil with good." Romans 12: 21

Lord – Today I sat next to a man who served in every war since Viet Nam - first as a medic on the front lines; and later as a doctor doing reconstructive surgery. He recently was shot in the arm over in Iraq and lost most of his muscle and use of his left hand. His career as a soldier and doctor came to an end. How did he respond? He now works on helping disabled vets retrain for new careers and he lobbies for education funding for vets. If we just open our eyes, we can see how you turn evil into good. For years this man worked to restore bodies. Now God is using him to restore human spirits. Let me have the faith, peace and courage of this soldier when I need evil to be turned into good.

Daily Prayer # 94

"Do not conform any longer to the pattern of this world, but be transformed by the renewing of your mind. Then you will be able to test and approve what God's will is – His good, pleasing and perfect will." Romans 12: 2

Lord – Sometimes my Christian walk feels like a dry desert place. I can't see You. I can't hear You. I can't feel your presence. I am tempted to believe that I am abandoned for a season, but I quickly resist those thoughts and claim Your promises. Thank You for the reality of Your word that keeps us grounded and our eyes upon You. Thank You for preparing me to face all circumstances and not be shaken by world events, work events, or personal events. Renew my mind today with Your thoughts and Your perfect will.

Daily Prayer # 95

"I wait for the Lord, my soul waits, and in His word I put my hope." Psalm 130: 5

Lord – There is refreshing in a desert place. When You allow circumstances to downsize our life – we get closer to You and closer to the ones we love. You are a good God to remind us what is really important. Help me to yield to Your will for my life and trust that You know what is best for me. I look forward to the outpouring that always follows a dry season. But I also want to appreciate, feed on Your word, and rest in this time of wait.

Daily Prayer # 96

"The hour has come for you to wake up from your slumber, because our salvation is nearer now than when we first believed. The night is nearly over, the day is almost here. So let us put aside the deeds of darkness and put on the armor of light." Romans 13: 11 – 12

Lord – I don't want to get to a point where I don't fight the good fight in prayer anymore. I don't want to become complacent and say, "My prayers don't matter. God will do what God will do." I don't want to be deceived by the enemy and fall asleep in the most important time in history. Just when we think all is lost – You show up on the scene. When breakthrough comes I want You to find me fighting. Renew my faith and spirit to fight for Your kingdom to be on earth.

Daily Prayer # 97

"I tell you the truth, unless you change and become like little children, you will never enter the kingdom of heaven. Therefore, whoever humbles himself like this child is the greatest in the kingdom of heaven." (Jesus) Matthew 18: 4 – 5

Lord – It is the hungry, the hurting, the sick, and the lost that are seeking answers and seeking You. The arrogant, self-sufficient and prideful do not want to know You. You truly came and died for all of us – but it is the least of us that find You and experience Your glory. Open my eyes to see the ones that need Your love the most and give me the love and resources to minister to them.

Daily Prayer # 98

"This is how my heavenly Father will treat each of you unless you forgive your brother from your heart." (Jesus) Matthew 18: 35

Lord – Help me to share a gospel of grace and forgiveness and not a gospel of rules and regulations. I try to live an obedient life because I love You. However, when I was lost I did not seek a righteous path – rather I sought and found Your love and forgiveness. Give me the grace to show that kind of love to people who are walking in disobedience. Always remind me that religion is not the path – Jesus is the path.

Daily Prayer # 99

"Do not be anxious about anything, but in everything, by prayer and petition, with thanksgiving, present your requests to God. And the peace of God, which transcends all understanding, will guard your hearts and your minds in Christ Jesus." Philippians 3: 6 – 7

Lord – "My conversations with You seem limited right now. In a waiting season, I don't have much to say. I want to choose my words wisely. If I don't have a heart of thankfulness, then I want to guard my lips. I don't want to put negative worries into the atmosphere because the enemy will use them against me. My silence is a caution to make all my words benefit me and those around me. Help me to proclaim the vision and promise even before it comes to pass. I will proclaim the goodness of the Lord and my words will be acceptable unto You.

Daily Prayer # 100

"Finally, brothers, whatever is true, whatever is noble, whatever is right, whatever is pure, whatever is lovely, whatever is admirable – if anything is excellent or praiseworthy – think about such things." Philippians 3: 8

Lord – My prayer is for those that have prayed these 100 prayers. Let the meditations of their hearts be acceptable unto You and may You give Your servants hope for their future. Let the words of Your promises and the encouragement of my messages stay sealed within their hearts to give the strength, joy, and peace in the days ahead. Do not let them be moved and help them to stand firm in what they first believed. Do not let them be deceived or become a part of the world. Keep them safe and protected in Your love.

 Workplace Wisdom

Double-Loop Thinking

"Great is our Lord and mighty in power; His understanding has no limit." Psalm 147: 5

When we come to a roadblock in our own personal lives and the old processes or ideas just are not working anymore, we usually quit trying to do it our way and take it to the Lord for an answer – a solution. God then reveals something we never thought about as a possibility.

When we struggle with decision "a" or decision "b" – the answer God gives us is usually decision "c" – a combination of the two or something entirely new. The same concept can be applied to projects and programs in the workplace. Looking at a whole new approach is called double-loop thinking.

Double-loop thinking is a quality control process where a team or leader takes a" double look" at the situation and questions the relevance of the existing way of doing things. Organizations willing to do this are called learning organizations.

Research on the success of double-loop thinking has caused many organizations to change their hiring process and find individuals who have a tendency and predisposition to double-loop think or "think outside the box" in order to stay competitive.

We can apply this to our own lives as leaders. Are we hanging onto old ways of doing things because of fear of losing a job assignment? Are we refusing to listen to the counsel of those younger than us who have a fresh view of the situation because of pride?

Stepping into a new realm can be a painful process of change for all – but the pain may prevent a crisis down the road.

Psalm 147: 6 says "The Lord sustains the humble." It takes humility to let go of old ways that are dear to us – but God will sustain us in the process. "

Daily Prayer # 101

"We have different gifts, according to the grace given us."
Romans 12: 6

Lord – Give me the grace to understand a diverse people and appreciate all the God-given gifts, talents and qualities you give each individual. Share with me Your wisdom that I may be the best example of acceptance and love to each individual. I am willing, God, – please make me able.

Daily Prayer # 102

"Be strong and courageous. Do not be terrified; do not be discouraged, for the Lord your God will be with you wherever you go." Joshua 1: 9

Lord – Whether in the workplace or in our families, we are all leaders. We are all models of excellence. It takes courage to make tough leadership decisions. Help me to overcome my fears of what others think and to focus on what is right. You are a just God. Let Your justice work through me when required and Your mercy when needed. May Jesus in me speak to others with words seasoned with grace just as He spoke to others when on the earth.

Daily Prayer # 103

"Serve one another in love. The entire law is summed up in a single command: 'Love your neighbor as yourself.'"
Galatians 5: 13 – 14

Lord – My mission is to love God and love people. My purpose is to serve others. Show me how I can produce fruit where you have me. Reveal to me how courageous Christianity translates into a love for You and Your people. As I yield this day to You let Your purposes be done through me.

Daily Prayer # 104

"Everything is possible for him or her who believes."
Mark 9: 23

Lord –You are Lord of time. If I focus on all my responsibilities, I become overwhelmed. If I focus on You, You manage my time. Help me achieve my goals and tasks today and throughout the week. Help me to listen to You and put first things first. Let Your peace and rest flow through me to others, even in the midst of chaos.

Daily Prayer # 105

"Do not confirm any longer to the pattern of this world, but be transformed by the renewing of your mind. Then you will be able to test and approve what God's will is – His good, pleasing and perfect will." Romans 12: 2

Lord – I want to make good decisions. I want to make decisions that produce results. Help me to trust that the creative thoughts that come to me are from You. Thank You for giving me answers in that same hour as I wait upon You for direction and timely answers to tough questions.

Daily Prayer # 106

"Be joyful always; pray continually; give thanks in all circumstances, for this is God's will for you in Christ Jesus." 2 Thessalonians 5: 16

Lord – Give me a cheerful spirit. Sometimes pain and tiredness can influence my countenance. I don't want others to see my pain or irritation. I want them to see the joy of the Lord in all circumstances. Being joyful in easy times does not demonstrate Your power. Being joyful when tired and stretched to the max shows how great You are. Let Your joy and power flow through me today.

Daily Prayer # 107

"I have told you these things, so that in Me you may have peace. In this world you will have trouble. But take heart! I have overcome the world." John 16: 33

Lord – How do those little "foxes" (thieves) sneak in? Before I know it, I am distracted by petty arguments, complaints and small issues that do not really matter in the big picture. I let go of these things today. I resist the enemy and know that he must flee. I choose to get back to trusting You and achieving my goals. I am focused again in Jesus' name!

Daily Prayer # 108

"Blessed are those who walk in the light of Your presence, O Lord. They rejoice in Your name all day long; they exult in Your righteousness." Psalm 89: 15 – 16

Lord – I am daily amazed at Your love for me. You accept me just the way I am. There is not one detail in my life that You don't care about. You hold up the universe and you hold up my life. How can such a big God care about such an insignificant person – but You do! Because of Your Son, Jesus, and the Holy Spirit, You are with me each and every hour. I draw from Your love and presence. You give me meaning for my life. You are why I can get up each day.

Daily Prayer # 109

"May the God of peace Himself give you peace at all times and in every way." 2 Thessalonians 3: 16

Lord – Sometimes it is easier to obey in action than to obey in thought. Jesus told us that our thoughts are important. I claim the mind of Christ today. I take captive in Christ every thought that does not align with the Word of God. I resist thoughts of unbelief, discouragement, weariness, covetousness, envy, strife, or jealousy. I bind Satan the thief from stealing my peace and joy. I proclaim the power of God's thoughts in my mind and I release any un-forgiveness in my heart. The mind of Christ is mine and I will rule with His authority, wisdom, power, and peace!

Daily Prayer # 110

"Everything is possible for him or her who believes." Mark 9: 23

Lord – There are so many movies, toys and images of dragons in this generation. I choose to let these images remind me that You are my *Dragon Slayer*. No matter how big and scary the situation, You have given me a shield of faith and the sword of the Spirit to overcome all circumstances. You also promise to fight those bigger battles for me. Thank you for slaying the "dragon of impossibilities" as I walk in faith with You.

✍ Workplace Wisdom

You Are Not Camping

"Thus says the Lord of hosts, the God of Israel, to all who were carried away captive, who I have caused to be carried away from Jerusalem to Babylon: Build houses and dwell in them; plant gardens and eat their fruit. Take wives and have sons and daughters . . .that you may be increased there, and not diminished" (Jeremiah 29: 4 – 6).

When the Israelites went into captivity in Babylon, they would wait for a message from the prophet Jeremiah who was still in Jerusalem. They were hoping for a message from God that said, "Keep your bags packed – you're coming back soon."

Instead they were given a marketplace message that they were going to be in Babylon for awhile, so they needed to make the best of it.

The letter from Jeremiah was suggesting: "You are not on a camping trip. This is your new home. Develop your community. Be productive. Cultivate where you are. Remember, your welfare is their welfare. Make the best of it. Develop wholeness and happiness and build a career of virtue. Find God in your current circumstances. Build houses. Grow gardens. Get married and have children."

God is telling us through this story that we need to "bloom where we are planted." We need to be productive and cultivate our skills. We also need to pray for our workplace and community because "their peace is our peace" (Jeremiah 29: 7)

What a powerful message that promotes the concept "God is Lord of business and the marketplace." God wants us to continue to serve and trust Him in our place of employment and in difficult situations.

Along with the discouraging message "be happy in your captivity" – Jeremiah also prophesied hope for the final outcome. In fact, a favorite and frequently quoted scripture is in this same letter sent to Babylon: "For I know the thoughts that I think toward you, says the Lord, thoughts of peace and not of evil, to give you a future and a hope. Then you will call upon Me and go and pray to Me, and I will listen to you" (Verses 11 & 12).

The situation was not to be forever, but in the meantime, they needed to get on with the normalcy of life. God's people were told that in 70 years they would be brought out of Babylon and returned to their homeland – and it happened as promised.

"Babylon workplace experiences" do not last forever. God always has a plan for good and for your future. Make a list of the "good things" you are getting from your work experience.

Reflect on all the skills you have learned and opportunities you have experienced over the past year or two. Now that you have "marked and acknowledged" this stage in your life, don't be surprised if the next path and journey is just around the corner. (I promise – it won't be 70 years).

Daily Prayer # 111

"Suddenly a great company of the heavenly host appeared with the angel, praising God and saying, 'Glory to God in the highest, and on earth peace to men on whom His favor rests.'" Luke 2: 13 - 14
Lord – You are a Lord of "suddenlies." I may be one decision, one prayer, one letter, one person, or one day away from a suddenly. Some people are one song or one book away from national and world-wide fame. We never know what tomorrow will bring and that is why we must be alert and full of expectation today. Help me in my hour of waiting. The time of the breakthrough is in Your hands. Help me to be prepared for the suddenly that is sure to come and arrive right on time.

Daily Prayer # 112

"Truly I tell you, whatever you forbid and declare to be improper and unlawful on earth must be what is already forbidden in heaven, and whatever you permit and declare proper and lawful on earth must be what is already permitted in heaven." Matthew 18:18 (Amplified)

Lord –Your Word is true and everything must agree with Your truth. It is hard for a human to believe in what we cannot see. Our flesh chases after circumstances and our hearts want to submit to the pain, sorrow, and suffering in ways that lead to our bondage. But I choose to follow You. I resist the enemy and declare Your works, I proclaim Your Word and thus walk in the Spirit. Strengthen me today to live according to Your Word. The Kingdom of God is at hand!

Daily Prayer # 113

"Praise God in His sanctuary; praise Him in His mighty heavens. Praise Him for His acts of power; praise Him for His surpassing greatness." Psalm 150: 1 – 2

Lord – Let the power of thanksgiving take over my life today. If one knee hurts, I will thank You for the knee that does not hurt. If one loved-one is unsaved, I will thank You for the one that is saved. If one bill is not paid, I thank You for the bills that are paid. If one person rejects me, I thank You for the ones who love me. If I lose a job, I thank you for the jobs had in the past and the jobs I will have in the future. You are my Healer, my Provider, my Friend, and my Destiny. Thank You for every gift from You that overflows into whatever I lack. Thank you for redeeming everything back to me.

Daily Prayer # 114

"No eye has seen, no ear has heard, no mind has conceived what God has prepared for those who love Him" I Corinthians 2: 9

Lord – There is always a "King Saul" or two in my life as there was in King David's. David was called by You, yet King Saul was jealous, David's wife was critical of him, and his son rebellious. Even during this discouraging circumstances, David always knew and trusted that God was in control of his destiny. He accepted the circumstances as God's will for his life. God used the accusations of others to build character and make him a patient leader. Help me to receive the training ground You have for me. Let me know when to be courageous, when to hold back, when to speak, when to be silent, when to call upon You to defend me, and when to accept with joy.

Daily Prayer # 115

"Let us hold unswervingly to the hope we profess, for He who promised is faithful. And let us consider how we may spur one another on toward love and good deeds." Hebrews 10: 23 – 24

Lord – Thank You for turning evil into good and working on our behalf. With God on our side no one can oppose or harm us. Whoever comes at us will fall away. Even the demons of hell will not prevail against us and they will bow down to the Lordship of Jesus in our lives. We are on the winning side! We know who defeated the enemy and we know who wins the battle. Hallelujah!

Daily Prayer # 116

"Come near to God and He will come near to you." James 4: 8

Lord – More of You and less of me – that is the only answer for success. Yet, I spend too little time in Your presence. I know what I should do but the cares of the world distract me. Forgive me and draw me back to the foot of the cross where I remember what this life is really all about. I love You Lord. I want to be with You now and forever. Thank you for always being with me.

Daily Prayer # 117

"God is able to make all grace abound to you, so that in all things at all times, having all that you need, you will abound in every good work." 2 Corinthians 9: 8

Lord – Help me find rest and joy in my work. It is becoming a burden rather than a mission. I know I must be stretched in my skills. When there is discomfort – there is growth. I don't want my days to just be one task after another – one challenge after another – or one test after another. I want to have mini miracles each and every day to remind me You are near. I want to share the gospel of love with someone who needs it. I pray that I will experience You in the midst of my daily work.

Daily Prayer # 118

"Let us fix our eyes on Jesus, the author and finisher of our faith . . ." Hebrews 12:2

Lord – Thank goodness I am not responsible to complete me! You are responsible. You are my Father God and You are raising me until the day of Christ Jesus. Help me to trust that I am exactly on the path at the place You want me. If I am behind, help me catch up. If I am ahead of You, help me slow down. If I am off track please bring me back on the path. Guide my footsteps each and every day.

Daily Prayer # 119

"Let your conversation be always full of grace, seasoned with salt, so that you may know how to answer everyone." Colossians 4: 6

Lord – Prior to this verse, Paul said to "be wise in the way you act toward outsiders, make the most of every opportunity." I think when we share with others we need to show genuine interest in them, be able to discuss intellectually things they are interested in, and share how Jesus has changed our life rather than preach at them. Help me to be a seed planter of love and interest as I share my light. Let my words be seasoned with salt.

Daily Prayer # 120

"Be on your guard; stand firm in the faith; be men and women of courage; be strong. Do everything in love." I Corinthians 16: 13 – 14

Lord – I need to pray for others more. Help me to be sensitive to other people's pains, insecurities or fears. Let me see beyond their temper, rudeness or coldness. Give me the courage to always reach out in love. Remind me to show acts of kindness to others and grant me the grace to not even notice the lack of kindness toward me. It only matters what *You* think of me – not how others respond. Let me be a child that reflects You.

 Workplace Wisdom

Passed Over

"For not from the east nor from the west nor from the south come promotion and lifting up, but God is the judge! He puts down one, and lifts up another" (Psalms 75: 6 & 7).

I have been passed over many times in the church and the workplace. I have often felt invisible at team meetings. I have watched others who have not demonstrated integrity, morality or fruits of the Spirit get chosen for leadership.

It can be very painful and confusing – but since my trust is in the Lord and not in man – I have learned to be at peace with it and know that in due time He will exalt me. He will know when I am ready.

Once in the past when I did not get a promotion that I was the most qualified for, a co-worker said, "Are you upset? I can't believe they did not choose you. Everyone is talking about it and in shock."

I replied, "That is very sweet – but my personal faith assures me that man can do nothing for me or against me that God does not approve in advance. I trust that He has a perfect plan for me and this was not it."

I love the story of Moses choosing the 70 elders to help him manage 600,000 men plus their wives and children. God came in a cloud and put the same Spirit that was on Moses on the elders (Numbers 11: 21 – 25).

The elders began to worship God and prophesy – declaring God's will. Back in the camp there were two men not chosen – but the Spirit fell on them too and they were worshiping and prophesying (Verses 26 – 28).

The people "tattled" and told Moses to stop them because "they were not chosen" – but Moses said, "Would that *all* the Lord's people were prophets and that the Lord would put His Spirit on them" (Verse 29).

You may be denied by men – but you will be declared by God and your gifts will come forth and be used in a mighty way in His time. I certainly can testify to that. Later, I was promoted to a senior executive in another company. The job that I didn't get a few years ago, no longer exists.

Is there someone in the workplace that keeps getting a promotion and favor that you envy? Give it over to God in prayer and don't let the seed consume your heart.

What do you do in the meantime? Document all your successes and achievements and keep your resume up to date. Do your part to look for job opportunities. When the right door opens – step through.

Daily Prayer # 121

"Jesus said, "Peace be with you! As the Father has sent me, I am sending you.' And with that he breathed on them and said, 'Receive the Holy Spirit.'" John 20: 21 & 22

Lord – I can't walk this journey without the Holy Spirit. I need the Teacher and the Comforter. I need the Wisdom and the Guidance. Breathe on me again and let the Holy Spirit fill me. Give me peace that only You can give; then let me pass that peace on to others.

Daily Prayer # 122

"Ask and it will be given to you; seek and you will find; knock and the door will be opened to you." Matthew 7: 7

Lord – I thank you that You are Lord of businesses, schools, governments, prisons, and nations. I thank You that You do not forsake us in whatever place we find ourselves. From the rising of the sun to the setting of the same You are attentive to our every heart's desire. All we need to do is ask. I seek You today for my family, for those around me, and for those in leadership over me. I know as I seek You, You will open doors for me.

Daily Prayer # 123

"You will be blessed when you come in and blessed when you go out. . . . Then all the peoples on earth will see that you are called by the name of the Lord, and they will fear you. The Lord will grant you abundant prosperity . . ."
Deuteronomy 28: 6, 10 – 11

Lord – I believe in your promises of an abundant life. I am opposed to a spirit of poverty. You were poor so that we could have according to Your word "all my needs met." Yes – there have been times of loss and times of mistakes on my part, but You have always provided and restored me to more than enough. Bless the work of my hands and bring increase for You are a God of increase.

Daily Prayer # 124

"Blessed are the poor in spirit, for theirs is the kingdom of heaven." Matthew 5: 1

Lord – Blessed are the poor in spirit for they shall see God. I was poor in my spirit when I did not know You. But now I am rich in faith and in Your love. There are so many poor-in-spirit-people in our families and around us. We have a gospel that can make the poor in spirit rich. Show me how to be generous with Your gift of faith and love and pour out this "wealth" to others.

Daily Prayer # 125

"My son (and daughter) preserve sound judgment and discernment, do not let them out of your sight; they will be life for you, an ornament to grace your neck." Proverbs 3: 21 – 22

Lord – Please be the Lord of all details in my life. Don't let any time be wasted. Rule in the hearts of men and women who make decisions on my behalf. Cause people to be teachable and receive Your instruction. Remove all strife and resistance. Please open doors that will bring success and close doors that will bring destruction. I give you the head seat at the table of all my decisions.

Daily Prayer # 126

"Finally, brothers and sisters whatever is true, whatever is noble, whatever is right, whatever is pure, whatever is lovely, whatever is admirable – if anything is excellent or praiseworthy – think about such things." Philippians 4: 8

Lord – Polish my heart. Remove old obstacles. Release me from thoughts of resistance, doubt or unbelief. Fill my heart with faith to believe that all things are possible. Clear the clutter from my mind so that I can focus on the pure and good. Release me to imagine great things that I can do today. Let a spirit of excellence be upon me.

Daily Prayer # 127

"'For my thoughts are not your thoughts, neither are your ways my ways', declares the Lord. 'As the heavens are higher than the earth, so are my ways higher than your ways and my thoughts than your thoughts.'" Isaiah 55: 8 & 9

Lord – You are a God who thinks outside the box. When we feel stuck You already see a way out. What we see as a rut is to You a waiting place. What we see as a mud pit You see an opportunity to mold a mountain. When we are entrenched in the world's economy You point us toward the Word-of-God economy. You are a creative God and Your mind and power is within me. I pray for wisdom and insight to see what you are doing through me and for me in all my circumstances.

Daily Prayer # 128

"We have this hope as an anchor for the soul, firm and secure." Hebrews 6: 19

Lord – When all is silent and nothing seems to be happening – fill me with hope that you are working behind the scenes. Hope says that eventually God will reveal His purpose, rescue me from the wilderness and set me on high. Hope says my God has been faithful in the past and therefore He will be faithful in the future. Hope says that during the storm, He will hold me secure.

Daily Prayer # 129

"All the days ordained for me were written in your book before one of them came to be." Psalm 139: 16

Lord – Expand my circle of influence where I have little or no control. Help me surrender to You when I fear the decisions of others that are in authority over me. Help me to grasp that You are in control. I trust You know what is best for me and You watch over the days ahead with great thoughtfulness and purpose.

Daily Prayer # 130

"If you have raced with men on foot and they have worn you out, how can you compete with horses? If you stumble in safe country, how will you manage in the thickets by the Jordan?" Jeremiah 12: 5

Lord – I want to run with horses. I want to be a swift steed – the head of the pack. Help me to run with men so that I will be ready to run with my horse assignments. I choose to stand my ground in trust and peace. I rest in You and know that You will be my strength and wisdom. I will not be moved in my soul but rather inspired in my spirit. I run the path you have before me and I choose this day to rest in You and not be worn out.

✍ Workplace Wisdom

Power – Not Pity

"I will sing of mercy and justice; to you, O Lord, I will sing praises. I will behave wisely in a perfect way, oh, when will You come to me? I will walk within my house with a perfect heart" (Psalm 101: 1 – 2).

In the late 1980s, I was President of the American Parents Association in Washington DC – fighting for moral values in public school legislation. One evening I felt sorry for myself and I called my husband from a Washington D.C. apartment crying about a personal minor conflict I had with a former Congressman. I was licking my wounds all alone in my apartment, wanting to be home with my family not in D.C.

I cried and complained to my husband, "Why is this happening to me? This is not fair." He calmly replied, "Because God is stretching you and preparing you?" I retorted in anger, "Well why isn't He stretching you? Why is it always *me*?" He calmly replied, "Because you are called to a great task and I am not."

I instantly stopped my pity party, because I knew he was right – but it certainly did not cure me forever. I have had multiple occasions of feeling that my trials are unjust and unfair compared to others.

On another trip in my current job I was in a corporate home in Texas while my husband resided in California. I called my husband and I began to cry and complain about my situation of once again being alone. Instead of being calm, this time he was firm, "Why do you let Satan do this to you? You keep listening to the same negative voices over and over again."

I wanted comfort and pity, but he wanted to get me back to a positive mental state. After we both got to a calm and sensible frame of mine, he said, "God does not always answer immediately but we have followed His direction and He has a plan.

We just need to go with the flow for now. As in the past, this part of the journey will eventually all become clear to us."

I then stirred myself up in the Lord to enjoy my children and grandchildren in Texas, study the Word, read some books, and write some devotions. There was more power in spending time with Jesus, then feeling sorry for myself.

What I discovered is that the pity party gave me no spiritual or emotional satisfaction. I did not feel better at the end of the day – I felt worse.

Just by thanking God for His goodness in specific areas of my life, I realized that there can be a quiet joy in knowing that He is a good God and only wants what is best for me – as a woman, as a wife, as a leader, and as His child.

Daily Prayer # 131

"I looked for a man among them who would build up the wall and stand before me in the gap on behalf of the land so I would not have to destroy it, but I found none." Ezekiel 22: 30

Lord – Through faithful prayers, I ask that you use me to fill the gaps in my family, in my workplace, and in my nation. Where there is strife, fill it with your peace. Where there is unkindness and jealousy fill it with Your love. Where there is confusion put things back in order. Where there is lack, fill it with your resources. Go before me as I pray for you to build up the walls of wisdom, moral values, and faith.

Daily Prayer # 132

"I know, my God, that you test the heart and are pleased with integrity. All these things have I given willingly and with honest intent. . . " I Chronicles: 29: 17

Lord - Don't let me get off track and compromise. Help me to stay on the high ground of all my decisions, thoughts and actions. As I run the race, let me be slow to listen, slow to respond, and slow to evaluate my choices. The slowness of pace and the waiting will enable me to hear your voice and to pay attention to the path before me.

Daily Prayer # 133

"You will not fear the terror of the night nor the arrow that flies by day." Psalm 91: 5

The rules are always changing around me in the game of life. Just when I think I understand the directions from those in authority, someone changes the rules. Thank goodness You are Lord of my game board. You know every "play" – every arrow - every penalty and even the toss of the die. Help me to know that wherever my steps lead me – there is only one direction – home – eternity with You.

Daily Prayer # 134

"Blessed are all who fear the Lord, who walk in His ways. You will eat the fruit of your labor, blessings and prosperity will be yours." Psalm 128: 1 – 2

I don't want to stop short of the blessing You have for me. I want to go one more mile. And at the end of the journey when I don't clearly see the results of my labor – I want to go one more mile again. Let me see this day as one more day in the center of your will and one more day closer to your purpose for me. You have something great for me to do and I may only be one day away. I give my all to you today and place the results and timing in your hands.

Daily Prayer # 135

"Today if you hear His voice, do not harden your hearts . . ." Hebrews 3: 8

Lord – Soft hearts are so important. Hard hearts make selfish decisions. Hard hearts create policies that make no sense and other people's lives difficult. A soft heart toward God is a teachable heart. Give me a soft heart. Help me to lead with the heart of God. Have mercy on me and help me to have mercy on others.

Daily Prayer # 136

"Cast your cares on the Lord and He will sustain you; He will never let the righteous fall." Psalm 55: 22

Lord – If I don't let go I can't move on. So I let go of poor decisions I made in the past. I let go of the pain others caused me and the pain I may have caused others. I let go of the wishing for a perfect job, perfect children, or a perfect marriage. I let go of the things I cannot change. I give it all to You and put my hope in You for better days ahead now that I am free and open to receive.

Daily Prayer # 137

*"Do not conform any longer to the pattern of this world;
but be transformed by the renewing o your mind. Then you
will be able to test and approve what God's will is – his
good, pleasing and perfect will." Romans 12: 2*

Let me have a mindset that thinks like You. I release the
old mindsets created by men or created by me. Let me
walk and make decisions according to your mindset. Let
me not be ashamed of Your Words and Your Ways. I pray
for courageous leadership that boldly goes in new ways
and direction according to Your perfect will.

Daily Prayer # 138

"Love must be sincere. Hate what is evil; cling to what is
good. Be devoted to one another in brotherly love. Honor
one another above yourselves." Romans 12: 9

Lord – Apart from love – nothing I do matters. Nothing I
achieve on will be proclaimed on Judgment Day. The only
thing you will ask is did we hate evil, cling to good, and
love others. Help me to stand against evil. Cause me to
always have a good work ethic and to be accountable for
my responsibilities. Remind me to love and honor others
in more than myself. I am humbled before You and yield
my self-will to You to do Your will.

Daily Prayer # 139

"Have mercy on me, O Lord, for I am weak; O Lord, heal me for my bones are troubled." Psalm 6: 2

Lord – Don't let the weariness of the day and the stress of the world get into my bones. I believe for your mercy and healing upon me and upon others today. I pray for a joyful heart, a joyful spirit, and joyful bones. The joy of the Lord is my strength so I choose to praise you and be thankful . Wrap your arms around me and carry the weariness on my behalf. I rest in your love.

Daily Prayer # 140

"The administration and the satraps tried to find grounds for charges against Daniel in his conduct of government affairs; but they were unable to do so. They could find no corruption in him because he was trustworthy and neither corrupt nor negligent." Daniel 6: 4

Lord – I wish I could say I have been as perfect as Daniel over the years but I cannot. I can say that I want to be as excellent as Daniel in all my ways so that those in authority over me and those beside me can find no fault with me. Holy Spirit, please help me to make a perfect decision in every situation and to walk in integrity with every minor detail. With the help of Jesus Christ within me, I will not compromise, I will not fail. I lean on you Lord to be a trustworthy worker and leader and to not be negligent with the tasks set before me. I commit my life, my leadership, and this day to You.

 Workplace Wisdom

Small Acts of Kindness

"For this very reason, make every effort to add to your faith goodness; and to goodness, knowledge; and to knowledge, self-control; and to self-control, perseverance; and to perseverance, godliness; and to godliness, brotherly kindness; and to brotherly kindness, love." 2 Peter 1: 5 – 7

One day I boarded an oversold, overcrowded, flight to San Francisco. Everyone scrambled to stow their luggage in a coveted overhead bin.

A woman in front of me was one of the last ones to drag her luggage down the aisle as she worked her way toward the last stand-by seat in front of me.

She struggled with her small bag, computer, and coat as she spotted a small spot left in the bin. Everyone stared at her as she seemed to take longer than necessary to figure out where to put everything and get seated.

I jumped up and said, "Here, let me hold your things while you get your bag in place." She gratefully handed me he coat and computer and caught my eyes for a split second to say a quick "thank you."

I found a place for her coat, waited for her to slide into her seat between two others, then handed her the computer and got myself re-settled.

She turned around and said, "I really needed someone to be kind to me today. I've had a terrible morning and everyone has been so unkind. Your act of kindness really encouraged me. Thank you."

The word *kindness* sort of hung in the air around everyone as if to say – "See how easy that was everyone. Pay attention more to each other."

I thought, "That was so easy – has the world really become so busy, so selfish, or so unhappy, there is no time for kindness?" In that moment I understood the power of "a simple act of kindness."

Jesus tells us to love our neighbor. Kindness is an action that demonstrates that love. We can impact our workplace and change the world one kindness at a time. We need to be reminded of the golden rule to treat others the way we want them to treat us.

Daily Prayer # 141

"Let the peace of Christ rule in your hearts, since as members of one body you were called to peace. And be thankful." Colossians 3: 15

Lord – When there is turmoil, fear, or strife in around me, I want to be Your vessel of peace. Use me to comfort, to calm, and to encourage others. Use me to help replace fear with hope and faith. I need Your wisdom to say the right words and the courage to step in where others fear to go. Change is hard and everyone reacts differently. I want to be Your voice of authority and peace in tough situations. I am willing to be a peacemaker if You will show me the way. Let Your peace be established in my surroundings today.

Daily Prayer # 142

"Whoever acknowledges Me before men, I will also acknowledge him before my Father in heaven." Matthew 10: 32

Lord – Wow! This is a tough one in a nation where the media turns people against Christians and people "don't want to hear it." I do not want to hold back out of fear. I do not want to be politically correct when it comes to Your kingdom. But I also want to be wise in all my ways. It would not bring you glory to get fired or start a fight. It does not bring glory to speak up when someone seeks help and prayer. Guide me in all my ways concerning this scripture and show me a balance that brings You glory and expands your kingdom here on earth. Thank you for the opportunity to share Your love with others and thank you for protecting me in those times. Guide my mouth and the testimony of my faith in Jesus' name.

Daily Prayer # 143

"Jesus looked at them and said, 'With man this is impossible, but not with God; all things are possible with God.'" Mark 10: 27

Lord – Sometimes I think I just don't have the skills and knowledge to advance any further. It would be easy for me to say "This is as far as I can go. This is the limit of the gifts and talents you gave me." But you want to stretch me even more and expand my territory. You want me to go the next step – the extra mile – because it is on that mile that you manifest Yourself through me. When we have no more strength and ability – Your strength and wisdom takes over. It is then we can give you the glory because it was impossible without You. Praise God for the impossible – for that is when I experience my Jesus.

Daily Prayer # 144

"Therefore I tell you whatever you ask for in prayer, believe that you have received it, and it will be yours. And when you stand praying, if you hold anything against anyone, forgive him or her, so that your Father in heaven may forgive you your sins." Mark 11: 24 & 25

Lord – I forgive all those who have hurt me . I forgive all those who have told lies about me. I forgive all those who have judged me wrongly. I forgive all those who walked over me on their way to the top. Thank You Lord for forgiving me and for hearing and answering my prayers. I come before You with a pure heart of forgiveness so that You can work through me. I submit to Your teaching of forgiveness in Your name. I believe.

Daily Prayer # 145

"For the Holy Spirit will teach you at that time what you should say." Luke 12: 12

Lord – I need the Holy Spirit in my conversations today. Sometimes I think of things too late to say. I need a timely word in the moment that I am asked. Reveal to my spirit and my mind those things that will make a difference, change a decision, or influence right choices. I want to be a mouthpiece for You. Open my spirit to hear the Holy Spirit more and more each and every day. I long to know Your voice more clearly when making decisions. Thank You for Your faithfulness to teach me what I should say.

Daily Prayer # 146

"I have told you these things, so that in Me you may have peace. In this world you will have trouble. But take heart! I have overcome the world." John 16: 33

Lord – Bad things do happen to good people. But in the midst of those trials and trouble – You have promised us peace! Not only have You promised us peace – but You have given us Your words to help us understand how we can overcome because You have overcome. I lift up my shield of faith and my sword of the spirit (the word of God) and stand with You today to overcome my circumstances. Help me to walk in steady peace and joy no matter where my path takes me. I rejoice at the steadfastness you have built within me with Your Word and the Holy Spirit. Jesus within me – be strong today.

Daily Prayer # 147

"Let nothing be done through strife or vainglory but in lowliness of mind let each esteem others better than themselves." Philippians 2: 3

Lord – Help me to remember that no matter what my title or education, we are all equal before You. I recall all those that have helped me on my journey. Use me to help others and remind me to appreciate the gifts I see in your creation. I know if I humble myself before You and trust You with my life, giving You the glory for everything, You will take care of my advancements and my promotions. With Your love in my heart, I can choose to honor and esteem others today.

Daily Prayer # 148

"Do all things without murmuring and disputing: That you may be blameless and harmless, the sons of God without rebuke, in the midst of a crooked and perverse nation, among whom you shine as lights in the world." Philippians 2: 14 – 15

Lord – When times are tough and people around me are in stress, it is so easy to get caught up in gossip and disputes. But that is not Your perfect will. Cause me to walk in the peace of your Word and to not criticize or condemn decisions that are being made. Rather use me as an influence of Your perfect ways to help calm those in need. Check my spirit quickly if I am tempted to participate in conversations that are not of You. Let me hear Your still small voice in the midst of a complex world.

Daily Prayer # 149

"Whatever you do, work at it with all your heart, as working for the Lord, not for men, since you know that you will receive an inheritance from the Lord as a reward. It is the Lord Christ you are serving." Colossians 3: 23 - 24

Lord – Thank you for the reminder that You are my boss! I choose to give 100% today to You. *You* see my hard work and faithfulness to do what is right and to treat others with respect and *You* will reward me and lift me up. I am thankful that You are a fair, just, and wonderful leader. Thank you Lord for being by my side as I do my tasks today.

Daily Prayer # 150

"I will rescue you from your own people and from the Gentiles. I am sending you to open their eyes and turn them from darkness to light, and from the power of Satan to God, so that they may receive forgiveness of sins and a place among those who are sanctified by faith in me." (Jesus) Acts 26: 17 & 18

Lord – Thank You for the death and resurrection of Your Son Jesus Who gives me salvation. I know I must do my part to obey Your Word and live a life of light and love. I also know that I cannot live that life without You – without prayer – and without reading the scripture. I acknowledge my weaknesses, but at the same time I pray for Grace to overcome. Let me be a light in the darkness and turn people to You.

 Workplace Wisdom

Lesson from a Horse

"Do not judge, or you too will be judged. For in the same way you judge others, you will be judged, and with the same measure you use, it will be measured to you" (Matthew 7: 1).

My dream is to have a leadership conference center where horses (and other animals) are a part of the leadership learning experience.

On a flight to Maryland, I sat next to an airline captain on her way back from a horsemanship training center in California. I showed her pictures of my six grandchildren and she showed me pictures of her three horses.

I asked her about horse training and she said that every horse has a different motivation that you need to discover to get them to respond. They either want safety, comfort, water, food, or kudus. It is rare, but a few horses perform just for the praise.

It reminded me of Maslow's Theory of Hierarchy of Needs that explains why people work. The lowest motivation is to eat and survive and the highest motivation is for personal satisfaction of achievement.

The airline Captain shared that horses want to please you, but we can't communicate effectively with them, so we have to discover what works by trial and error. There are a lot of things a horse can't do for itself and it is dependent on the trainer for direction. Once the horse trusts the trainer, it is easier to communicate. When the horse finally understands what you want, it is rewarded for the right action, and gets it. When the horse finally understands, there is an actual sign of relief on the horse and a display of less stress, less resistance, and more confidence.

This concept is similar to situational leadership. In the beginning with a new employee or new assignment – more time needs to be spent on giving directions and ensuring that there is clarity in the communication. Through reward and recognition, the employee gradually moves in a direction of more into independence and high performance.

Jesus was always asking people "What do you want me to do for you?" or asking His disciples, "What are you thinking right now about this?" Even though He had authority and power – He was always asking instead of telling.

Think about your employees or team members as individuals. Find out what motivates them – what worries them – or why they took the job. Discover what their career goals are and pray about what you can do to help get them there.

Good leaders motivate others by their listening skills. Listen and then act on what you hear.

Daily Prayer # 151

"And without faith it is impossible to please God, because anyone who comes to Him must believe that He exists and that He rewards those who earnestly seek Him." Hebrews 11: 6

Lord – What is the balance between faith in You and doing my part? How do we know when to wait and when to step out in faith and take action? I guess I have to do what seems right and trust that You will stop me if it is wrong. Holy Spirit, turn my 'radio channel' to the right frequency to hear the voice of my Lord. If I don't know what to do I will wait and pray and seek You with all my heart.

Daily Prayer # 152

"Endure hardship with us like a good soldier of Christ Jesus. No one serving as a soldier gets involved in civilian affairs – he wants to please his commanding officer." 2 Timothy 2: 3 & 4

Lord – I am waiting on Your orders. I feel like I am marching in place. There is no movement in any direction. There must be a reason for soldiers marching in place. Is it to keep the energy going until the next marching order? Is it to make sure we don't fall asleep and give up on the dream? Is it to let the enemy know we are still here ready to do battle? Is it to wait for the other troops to join us? Or is it to stay alert, prepared and ready? Help me to praise You and not complain about marching in place.

Daily Prayer # 153

"But those who hope in the Lord will renew their strength." Isaiah 40: 31

Lord – I thank you for seasons. It reminds me that there are seasons in my life. The best season is spring when we get to start something new and we celebrate the resurrection of Jesus Christ. Winter is not my favorite – but it is a time to reflect on You and renew my strength. Help me to trust that all seasons have a purpose and to remember that even in the winter season you are nourishing my soul and causing my roots to go down deep to prepare for all the new growth that is about to take place.

Daily Prayer # 154

"He has taken me to the banquet hall and His banner over me is love." Song of Solomon 2: 4

Lord –I am looking forward to the big banquet party in heaven, but I am determined that as long as I am here on earth, I will celebrate Your love. Fill my heart with joy. You alone can make us lighthearted in a heavy and troubled world. Let others see my joy and be drawn to You.

Daily Prayer # 155

"Whatever you do, work at it with all your heart, as working for the Lord, not for men, since you know that you will receive an inheritance from the Lord as a reward." Colossians 3: 23 & 24

Lord – Work is important to You. You provide for us through work. It is our gifts and talents that help us find our niche in the world. I sometimes wish that money supernaturally dropped from Heaven – but it doesn't. Yet I know if I keep up my training and keep my heart and mind open to change – there will always be a place for me to work. You open the door – I will walk through to the other side.

Daily Prayer # 156

"When my life was ebbing away, I remembered You, Lord, and my prayer rose to You, in Your holy temple." Jonah 1: 7

Lord – Sometimes there are things I just can't do anything about. I struggle to fix it or change it or speed it up. But it doesn't budge. I give those things to You. I ask for your ministering angels to go before me and accomplish your will in the tasks I cannot do. I release all barriers into your hands. Not in my timing - but in Your time.

Daily Prayer # 157

"From inside the fish Jonah prayed to the Lord his God.
He said: . . . with a song of thanksgiving, with sacrifice to
you. What I have vowed I will make good. Salvation
<deliverance> comes from the Lord." Jonah 2: 1 and 9.

Lord – How I am reminded that I am to praise You in the
midst of my circumstances! Even in the darkness of the
belly of a whale, I am to sing songs of thanksgiving and
literally sacrifice my worship to You. Only in the midst of
praise will You deliver us. It is the songs of thanksgiving
that breaks the yoke of bondage. I glorify You today and
recognize You as the Almighty God who with Sovereignty
guides my life.

Daily Prayer # 158

"Before I formed you, in the womb I knew you, before you
were born I set you apart; I appointed you as a prophet to
the nations." Jeremiah 1: 5

Lord – Forgive me for comparing myself to others. I often
think others are more equipped or more suited to do the
tasks you have assigned me. Help me to remember that I
am unique and created for a special purpose. The person I
am now – my age, my education, and my personality – are
perfect for what You have planned for me because You
decided when you created me that I would be just as I am
at this time in history. I will be the best that I can be for
You.

Daily Prayer # 159

"The Lord remembers us and will bless us; He will bless the house of Israel, He will bless the house of Aaron, He will bless those who fear the Lord – small and great alike. May the Lord make you increase, both you and your children. May you be blessed by the Lord, the Maker of heaven and earth." Psalm 115: 12 – 15

Lord – Thank you that Jesus broke the curse that was on us from Adam and now the blessing of Abraham is upon me and my family, my animals, my household, my marriage, and my workplace. I walk in Your blessing today – every day – and receive all the good things You have planned for me.

Daily Prayer # 160

"Surely, goodness and love <mercy> will follow me all the days of my life, and I will dwell in the house of the Lord forever." Psalm 23: 6

Lord – This scripture means that each and every day You are chasing after me with your goodness and love. What can man do to me when You are following me with Your blessings? You see everything and You will keep me out of harms' way. Your glory is my rear guard of protection.

✍ Workplace Wisdom

The Path to God's Heart

"Whatever you did for one of the least of these – you did for me" (Matthew 25:40).

Do you realize it is very easy to please God? Some of us may think it is necessary to complete a long list of accomplishments in order to reach His heart – but God sent His Son to tell us a simple message - "Love God and love our neighbor" (Luke 10:27). Jesus teaches his disciples to reach out to those in despair, poverty, loneliness, or hopelessness.

When my husband worked in Portland, Oregon, he would often go for walks on his lunch break along the Willamette River. One day he heard the Lord speak to him gently in his heart. That evening, he told me with excitement, "I heard the Lord tell me that He is pleased with us."

I couldn't wait to discover why God was so proud of us. I asked, "What did He say? What pleases Him?" He replied, "He thanked us for caring about the least of His." I replied, "I don't understand."

My husband explained how pleased the Lord was that we had let three homeless women on three different occasions live in our home; how we had shared our home and limited resources with foreign exchange students so they could experience America; and how we cared for hurt and abandoned animals. Finally, the Lord was pleased at how we welcomed the neighborhood children into our home sharing time and love.

In my youth and amazement, I asked, "That's it? That's what impresses the Lord?" I sat in wonderment at how simple it really was to please God.

My husband and I refer to those days as our "season of poverty." But now I realize how rich we really were.

The greatest struggle many of us have today with giving, serving, and charity is lack of time or resources. We are convinced that our schedules are so extremely busy and our finances so tight that we don't have time or money for anyone but our jobs and our families.

I am of the theory that when we give of our time and resources, _we gain time and resources_. The investment will never rob us – it will increase us both on earth and in heaven.

Jesus was moved by compassion, not by obligation or desire for advancement. What moves you?

Daily Prayer # 161

"He will make your righteousness shine like the dawn, the justice of your cause like the noonday sun." Psalm 37: 6

Lord – Every day is a new day. Your creativity is limitless so each day is never the same. Make this day a special day for me. Let me see You in new ways. Surprise me with a gift – a touch of You that lifts my spirits. Open my eyes to see the little things you do for me. Use me to do little things for others.

Daily Prayer # 162

"Blessed is the man who finds wisdom, the man who gains understanding, for she is more profitable than silver and yields better returns than gold. She is more precious than rubies; nothing you desire can compare with her." Proverbs 3: 13 – 15

Lord – I notice when the light goes through my ring it reflects many facets of light on the wall. If it was not a clear diamond, the light would be reduced. I come to you and ask forgiveness. I ask You to clean my vessel and keep my heart pure so that Your light can shine though. I thank You that Jesus Christ is my inner light and magnifies Your love through me.

Daily Prayer # 163

"In repentance and rest is your salvation; in quietness and trust is your strength." Isaiah 30: 15

Lord – I repent of worry. I am sorry that I think too much about the future and don't rest in the present. I rise early in the quietness of the day so that I can be quiet in your presence and spend time building my trust in Your Word. I chose to take the time to lean on You for strength today.

Daily Prayer # 164

"Being strengthened with all power according to his glorious might so that you may have great endurance and patience, and joyfully giving thanks to the Father who has qualified you to share in the inheritance of the saints in the kingdom of light." Colossians 1: 11

Lord – Of all the fruits of the spirit we are to practice, You seem to always bring us back to patience. Whether we are standing in faith for answer to prayer, an improved relationship, or waiting on You for revelation of the next step - it always takes patience. Strengthen me to not give up too soon. Don't let me quit just moments before the answered prayer. Let me cross the finish line into Your promises. Help me to patiently wait for what I cannot yet see.

Daily Prayer # 165

"And God is faithful; He will not let you be tempted beyond what you can bear. But when you are tempted, He will also provide a way out so that you can stand up under it." I Corinthians 10: 13

Lord – I am encouraged to realize that testing is not to bring us to our knees in discouragement and defeat. It is for the growing of our faith. You don't allow the tests and trials to teach us a lesson but rather to grow us. You permit the tests in this world so that we will use our weapons of prayer, faith, fasting, courage, and patience to be overcomers in this world. It is not the tests and trials that prepare us – but rather the faith and endurance we use in those trials. It is Your promise to not forsake us that we must focus on – not the trial.

Daily Prayer # 166

"With the tongue we praise our Lord and Father, and with it we curse men, who have been made in God's likeness. Out of the same mouth come praise and cursing. My brothers and sisters, this should not be." James 3: 9 – 10

Lord – I must continue to learn to align my tongue with what I believe is going to come to pass. If I am not talking about the vision You gave me, then I am doubting Your promises. If I am confessing negative then I am contradicting Your word. Holy Spirit, help me to walk in accordance with God's will for my life and to speak words of agreement, belief, and trust. Jesus said that He only speaks what the Father tells Him. I want to be more like Jesus.

Daily Prayer # 167

"Let us not become weary in doing good, for at the proper time we will reap a harvest if we do not give up."
Galatians 6: 9

Lord – No matter how far I have come in my spiritual growth there is still much further to go. I need a "marking point" that shows me where I am on your measuring stick for the earthly plan of my life. It seems like such a slow journey with so many lessons to learn. Help me to know that I have progressed on Your timeline and that we are right on schedule. It is so hard to understand why evil men rule and wicked leaders advance while Your people are hidden in the background. But I will remember to not envy evil men and to not grow weary in well doing.

Daily Prayer # 168

"If I speak in the tongues of men and angels, but have not love, I am only a resounding gong or a clanging cymbal."
I Corinthians 13: 1

Lord – When people revile me or speak evil of me for no just cause - I must have love. When leaders or people around me make mistakes that impact me - I must respond in love. I must respond in the same way Jesus responds to me - with love. I must apply the same grace that I have been shown. Give me the gift of leading with love. Give me the grace to overcome the temptation of anger and frustration. Give me the wisdom to lead people in truth and love as Jesus led His disciples.

Daily Prayer # 169

"The Lord will guide you always; He will satisfy your needs in a sun-scorched land and will strengthen your frame." Isaiah 58: 11

Lord – Thank you that You are like a refreshing stream on a hot Summer day. Thank You that Your Spirit restores my soul. Let others see Your refreshing peace in my life so that I can pour out Your love and kindness to them. As You are a cup of cold water to me, let me be a cup of cold water to others today. And thank you dear Lord that "my frame" – my bones – shall be strong in You and I will not be weary.

Daily Prayer # 170

"All your sons will be taught by the Lord, and great will be your children's peace." Isaiah 54: 13

Lord – Thank you for your promise that if I serve Your children in the Body of Christ You will take care of my children. If I put You first in my life – You will take care of everything that is dear to me. Your hand of love and protection upon my family blesses my heart. I send Your peace to my children in Jesus' name. This gives me great comfort so that I can focus on the tasks You have set before me.
Reflection:

Workplace Wisdom

Showroom Christians

Not that I have now attained (this ideal), or have already been made perfect, but I press onto lay hold of (grasp) and make my own, that for which Christ Jesus (the Messiah) has laid hold of me and made me His own. Philippians 3:12

After many years of trying to be a "good Christian," I finally figured out that Wendy could not do it, and I had to let Jesus be a Christian through me. God does not want perfect Christians to put in a showroom for all to see. Instead, the only perfection we should be working on is our perfection with our relationship with Jesus.

There was one point in my life that I was broken and ashamed of my failure as a Christian. I was completely empty inside and felt like I would never have anything to give God again. In fact, I could not even imagine why He would even want to use me.

An evangelist looked at me one day in a prayer meeting and said, "Your vessel is completely drained out and empty, isn't it?" I said with tears in my eyes, "Yes."

"Good!" he exclaimed! "Now God can finally pour Himself in you and use you!"

A short time later I won a school board election, wrote a book on school boards, and traveled to 44 states giving school board training workshops. An organization evolved called The American Parents Association. Its member's lobbied schools and legislatures for local control, parent rights, and morally sound curriculum.

I spoke on multiple radio and TV stations including an interview on the Today show with Katie Couric. It is estimated that at least 2000 Christians or political conservatives won their school board elections as a result of a four year ministry.

If we dwell in Him, His characteristics will begin to pour out of us, and others will be drawn to HIM because of this relationship – not because of our so-called perfect Christianity. In fact, it is Christians judging others in the Christian showroom that is driving people away from God today.

People are hungry for something real, relevant, and loving in their lives and only Jesus can give that. Spend time with God in the morning, and then let Him be real, relevant, and loving to others through you throughout the day. My prayer is to not be "full of myself" but to be full of God.

Daily Prayer # 171

"As for me, far be it for me that I should sin against the Lord by failing to pray for you." I Samuel 12:23

Lord –Even if I don't agree with my spouse, boss, or pastor, far be it for me that I fail to pray for them. It is your desire that we live a life of prayer for others. Make it my desire too.

Daily Prayer # 172

"Is the Lord's arm to short? You will now see whether or not what I say will come true for you." Numbers 11:23

Lord – Moses questioned how You would give meat to thousands of Israelites in the desert. You sent the quail to feed them. We sometimes wonder how Moses doubted anything after the parting of the Red Sea. With Jesus's help within me, I choose to believe You will meet all my needs. I choose to believe that Your arm is not too short to save, to provide, to protect, and to heal. I rebuke the spirit of unbelief that keeps attacking me and Your people. Help me to continue to keep my eyes on You and upon Your promises.

Daily Prayer # 173

"My Presence will go with you and I will give you rest."
Exodus 33:14

Lord – This is a wonderful two-fold promise. Your Presence will give me energy, purpose, and direction. In addition and at the same time, it will give me rest. As I read our word and pray, I want to feel your presence. But more important is that others will feel your presence as I pray for them and know that you are alive and real. Let Your presence go with me today.

Daily Prayer # 174

"Then they understood that He was not telling them to guard against the yeast used in bread, but against the teaching of the Pharisees and Sadducees." Matthew 16: 12

Lord – Protect me from legalism and the laws of man-made religion. Always remind me that it is Jesus "plus" nothing. It is by grace that I am saved, not by works. Jesus accepted me just the way I was. I want to be used by You to accept others and show them Your Mercy.

Daily Prayer # 175

"The salvation of the righteous comes from the Lord; He is their stronghold in times of trouble." Psalm 37: 39

Lord – What a wonderful thought. Just like in battle, when there is a stronghold of soldiers who have secured a territory, the enemy cannot get in. You are encompassed round about me and You will keep me safe. No weapon formed against me shall prosper. It will be a "missile dud" that falls to the ground. You will extinguish any fiery darts that are shot in my direction. Even if everything and everyone around me is in chaos – I will stand in peace.

Daily Prayer # 176

"I was young and now I am old yet I have never seen the righteous forsaken or their children begging bread. They are always generous and lend freely; their children will be blessed." Psalm 37: 25 & 26

Lord – I send this message out to all my friends who are parents to assure them that You take care of our children. We have this promise not because of our works but because of your love, grace and mercy. Bless me also with the promise that I and my children will always be generous and lend freely. Thank you.

Daily Prayer # 177

"With long life will I satisfy him and show him my salvation." Psalm 91: 16

Lord – A lot of people talk about going to heaven or want Jesus to come back soon. But I think in Your heart You want us to live as long as possible to share Christ with as many of your children as possible before the end of time. I want to live a long life and I want to be part of the great harvest that you have promised through Your prophets. Open many more doors for me to share Your love and to explain the good news of Jesus Christ.

Daily Prayer # 178

"Even in darkness, light dawns for the upright, for the Lord is gracious and compassionate." Psalm 112: 4

Lord – Let your light shine on me. Let Your graciousness be present in my life. Let Your compassion fill my heart. Let Your righteousness guide me. It is through this testimony of Your light and presence that others can see You. May Your light dawn upon us all.

Daily Prayer # 179

"May the Lord make You increase, both You and Your children." Psalm 114: 14

Lord – You desire increase – not decrease. You want us to take the land – not shrink back. You want us to prosper – not live in poverty. You want our children and grandchildren blessed – not cursed. You want to expand our territory – not limit our boundaries. I open my mind, heart, and spirit to receive Your increase.

Daily Prayer # 180

"Do not withhold good from those who deserve it, when it is in your power to act." Proverbs 3: 27

Lord – Thank you for all the opportunities You have given me in the past and will give me in the future to help those in need. If someone at work needs a word of encouragement or a free lunch, show me who they are. I resist the temptation of being too thrifty or too busy to meet the needs of others.

 Workplace Wisdom

Pick Up the Towel

"Now that I, your Lord and Teacher, have washed your feet, you also should wash one another's feet." John 12:14

This is verse is a message about the daily tasks in our lives. Sometimes I think, "When I am the leader of my own organization, I'm going serve like this." God says, "You need to not wait and start serving now." He wants us to pick up the towel, wash feet, and serve others in menial tasks right where we are. How we serve today is an indication of how we will lead tomorrow.

I like being a leader more than a manager. A leader gets to inspire, create vision, and be a change agent. A manager has to manage operations, budgets and the conflicts of people. After a challenging week of problem solving, I drove home one evening and said, "I don't want to do this Lord – I don't enjoy it. I just want to move on to greater things."

Do you know what He said in my spirit immediately? "Grow up." Honest! He said, "Grow up and face your responsibilities. You cannot be a leader without being a manager. There will always be seasons of these tasks, challenges and pressures. If you can't handle this – you are not going to be able to handle the next step I have for you."

I now receive my challenges as training gifts from God. Our mundane tasks and responsibilities are God's training ground in our lives. He engineers them to get us ready. Jesus calls it "picking up the towel."

Daily Prayer # 181

"Even Elizabeth your relative is going to have a child in her old age, and she who was said to be barren is in her sixth month. For nothing is impossible with God." Luke 1: 36 & 37

Lord – Thank you for the reminder that I am never too old to work for You and that it is never too late for the dream to come to pass. You do like to work in impossible situations so I give all my impossibilities to You.

Daily Prayer # 182

"Many are the plans in a man's heart, but it is the Lord's purpose that prevails." Proverbs 19: 21

Lord – I have so many ideas and I see so many opportunities – but I only want to pursue Your purpose for my life. Let all the plans that are not of You fall away and show me the ones that will prevail and achieve Your destiny for me. Order my footsteps and show me the path. Open the door and I will do my part and walk through in obedience.

Daily Prayer # 183

"This is what the Sovereign Lord, the Holy One of Israel says: 'In repentance and rest is your salvation; in quietness and trust is your strength.'" Isaiah 30: 15

Lord – I must completely let go of the trying to control the plan. In quietness and trust I will see You take hold. Even when government or workplace leaders make confusing decisions, Your hand is upon me and I will not be moved by discouragement or fear. Your angels are encompassed around me and You alone are my shield against the fiery heat of fear, oppression, persecution, or drought. You bring me living waters in the desert and I will rest by your stream of hope.

Daily Prayer # 184

"Yet the Lord longs to be gracious to you; he rises to show you compassion. For the Lord is a God of justice. Blessed are all who wait for Him!" Isaiah 30: 18

Lord – Thank you for hearing our prayers and longing to be gracious to us and show us blessing, compassion, and justice. Help me to wait patiently for the timing of answered prayer. Let the word of God build that patience for your promises within me. Thank You for Your loving-kindness toward me and cause me to quietly wait in Your presence for answers and direction.

Daily Prayer # 185

"To whom will you compare Me? Or who is My equal?"
Isaiah 40: 25

Lord – Nothing compares to You. Not silver, gold, or diamonds hold up to your glory. Not success or worldly riches give me life satisfaction the way You do. You alone are the center of my thoughts and actions. As I seek you, all my needs will be met for You are my Source. I will have the wisdom I need, the grace I need, the compassion I need, and the strength I need to perform my tasks and lead others. I receive Your blessing in my life.

Daily Prayer # 186

"To him who is able to keep you from falling and to present you before his glorious presence without fault and with great joy." Jude 24

Lord – I am so thankful that You will finish what You began in me on that day I accepted You into my heart and made you Lord of my life. You pick me up when I fall down. You bring me closer and closer to the reflection of Jesus Christ. You are faithful to continually guide me and grow me. Your mercy endures forever.

Daily Prayer # 187

"As the rain and the snow come down from heaven, and do not return to it without watering the earth . . . so is the Word that goes out from My mouth. It will not return to Me empty, but will accomplish what I desire and achieve the purpose for which I sent it." Isaiah 55: 10 & 11

Lord – Water my prayers and seeds of light and love so that a harvest may bloom. Whenever I share Your Words of wisdom, truth, or peace with someone, let it accomplish good things in that person's life. Be faithful to send someone to water those seeds. Let the Words that I have been studying birth a harvest of truth and strength within my soul.

Daily Prayer # 188

"He reveals deep and hidden things; He knows what lies in darkness, and light dwells with Him." Daniel 2: 22

Lord – Daniel completely trusted you to reveal the interpretation of the dream. He knew You were the source of all knowledge and wisdom. Help me to remember what a mighty God we serve. You alone have all the answers to our questions. You can see the big picture and You know what the future holds. I am so glad that I serve a God of light who dispels all the darkness.

Daily Prayer # 189

"Those who cling to worthless idols forfeit the grace that could be theirs." Jonah 2:8

Lord – I want no other gods before you. I want You first in my life, first in my career, and first in my day. I choose to spend time in Your word and to spend time in ministry that expands Your kingdom. As I think about how I can serve others each day – You will take care of the details of my day. Remind me each day that my primary purpose in life is to share the good news of Your love with others. Thank you for the grace that is in my life because I chose to cling to You. Tomorrow and the days ahead, I will put you first.

Daily Prayer # 190

"It is not the healthy who need a doctor, but the sick. But go and learn what this means: 'I desire mercy, not sacrifice.' For I have not come to call the righteous, but sinners." Matthew 9: 12

Lord – Thank you for the reminder that we are here for the sick, hurting, lost, poor, homeless and prisoner. It is only because of your mercy that I am saved – not any good works. Give me a heart of love and forgiveness for EVERYONE that crosses my path. The simple message "God loves you" needs to be heard by all. I want to be that messenger in words and action.

 Workplace Wisdom

Message from a Friend

I want to share with you a message I was given in 1986, written by a friend who was dying of cancer.

"Quit complaining about who you are or your lack of skills. If the Lord had wanted you to be different He would have done so back when you were being formed.

Can you accept that He hasn't overlooked a thing? For He has promised to make all things, including our own wrong choices, work out for good when we trust Him.

As you thank God for every difficulty, submitting to His will at every turn, He is able to move us into the spot where He wants us.

Your task is to thank Him for where you are at present. Whatever happens continue to thank Him – for He is in charge."

Daily Prayer # 191

"For nothing is impossible with God." Luke 1: 37

Lord – Help me to not put limits on You with my limited thinking. Give me eyes to see what You can do and want to do. Give me eyes to see a dream fulfilled, a healed relationship, a revival in our nation, bodies made whole, the captive set free and prayers answered. Lift my eyes up off of my circumstances and onto you and Your son, Jesus. Lord, give me a larger portion of faith to know that nothing is impossible. I want to start declaring Your promises and vision today.

Daily Prayer # 192

"Jesus Christ is the same yesterday, today, and forever." Hebrews 13: 8

Lord –This is one of Your most powerful scriptures. It says to me that the Bible stories and promises are all true. The Old Testament prophets directed us to Jesus; the miracles you did for Joseph, Ester, and Daniel, You will do for us today; the demonstration of Your love and power while Jesus walked the earth is with us now; and all of these promises will be with us in the future wherever our journey takes us. Thank you Jesus for not changing and for being steadfast and faithful to me. Help me to remain steadfast and faithful to You. Just as You walked with the disciples, walk with me. Demonstrate Your peace and power through me to others.

Daily Prayer # 193

"Your prayers and gifts to the poor have come up as a memorial offering before God." Acts 10: 46

Lord – Even in our most desperate times there is always someone in greater need than me. Remind me to focus on the needs of others and to give my personal needs to You. Know that giving to the poor is "a memorial to You" is a huge blessing to my heart. Show me how to also give to the spiritual poor around me. Let me be a cup of refreshing water to those that thirst.

Daily Prayer # 194

"How beautiful are the feet of those who bring good news." Romans 10: 15

Lord – I don't want to deliver bad news, economic news, sad news, or angry news. I want to be the bearer of good news – good news that ministers to people's hearts and minds. The best news of all is to tell people (and show people) that God loves them. Give me opportunities to share good news today. Stop me if I am about to say anything negative that does not glorify God.

Daily Prayer # 195

"Do not conform any longer to the pattern of this world, but be transformed by the renewing of your mind. Then you will be able to rest and approve what God's will is - His good, pleasing and perfect will." Romans 12: 2

Lord - As I read Your Word, my mind becomes transformed and aligned with Your will. Help me to make decisions in accordance with Your Will and Your Word and not in accordance with the pattern of this world. I want to be a Joseph, Nehemiah, Daniel, and Esther in the workplace. I want to be tuned in to Your voice and direction and follow Your good, pleasing, and perfect will for my life and for the lives of others. I chose to enter a rest and be guided by You and Your Words that are blossoming within me.

Daily Prayer # 196

"I pray not that Thou should take them out of the world, but that Thou should keep them from evil." John 17: 15

Lord –You want to be with me in the midst of my circumstances. Thank you, Jesus, for asking the Father to keep evil from me. Thank you that you defeated Satan at the cross. Because of You, I have the authority to walk in peace and safety in the midst of the darkness that surrounds me. Give me victory today over every situation. Give me success today. Give me wisdom today. And keep evil from me.

Daily Prayer # 197

"Death and life are in the power of the tongue and they that live it shall eat the fruit thereof." Proverbs 18: 21

Lord – Put a guard at my mouth and only let me speak words of life. Let the words of my mouth be acceptable unto You. Let the words of prayer I speak over others be a life changing force, and may Your wisdom spoken through me accomplish great things for Your kingdom and Your glory.

Daily Prayer # 198

"For as he thinks in his heart so is he." Proverbs 23: 7

Lord – The enemy attacks through the mind and it is the mind that can guide me into wrong decisions, fears, or doubt. I receive the mind of Christ today to think like You, plan like You, talk like You, and believe like You. I refuse to let the enemy bring fear through my mind when I know in my heart that You are already victorious in my life.

Daily Prayer # 199

"The steps of a good man are ordered of the Lord." Psalm 37: 23

Lord – Our days are numbered by You. There is a path that you have set before us to complete. If I am off the path, reveal to me the errors of my ways and get me back on track. Help me to walk by faith and know when to walk, when to run, and when to wait. I want You to order my footsteps every day.

Daily Prayer # 200

"Now as He drew near, He saw the city and wept over it, saying, 'If you had known, even you, especially in this your day, the things that make for your peace! But now they are hidden from your eyes.'" Luke 19: 41

Lord – You wept over blind eyes, hard hearts, and lost souls. Souls are so valuable. You died for souls and Satan fights to steal souls. I am sorry that I often take my Salvation for granted and forget to share the gospel with others. Give me your heart for lost souls and give me opportunity to share the message of forgiveness and hope with others. I am available – make me courageous and capable.

 Workplace Wisdom

I Know Your Voice

"Commit your works to the Lord, and your thoughts will be established. . . A man's heart plans his way, but the Lord directs his steps." Proverbs 16: 3 &9

My daughter says to me, "Mom, when you leave a voicemail you don't need to say 'this is mom' – I know your voice."

It made me think about the question, "How do you know God's voice?" To me, it's obvious from my daughter, the message is: "the more time you spend with Him, the more you know His voice" (John 16: 27 & 28).

Part of knowing God's voice is knowing that the direction we are hearing in our hearts and minds aligns with the character of God. The character of God is full of peace, not stress or strife; the character of God is gentle, not forceful; and the character of God is having a sound mind, not confusion.

Direction and decisions that are of God are clear, concise, and full of peace – even in the midst of a crisis. You don't have to force yourself to go in the direction you are being guided in – you *know* that it is right. The thoughts that you get to quickly solve problems are more than likely from Him. Why? Because He said he will be faithful to order the steps of the righteous.

I was asked by my students at Biola University if my direction and wisdom to make leadership decisions came from the Holy Spirit or from my education and training. I have to say "both." God is a Spirit but He is also a practical God – or he would not have used a construction worker to restore the wall in Jerusalem. The Holy Spirit combines the word of God and our faith with our experiences and practical knowledge, stirs it in a bowl, and it comes out *WISDOM*.

All the training, all the preparation, all the coaching and counseling from other leaders, all the reading of the Bible and business books, and all the praying, has been God's voice into my life because I TRUST that according to His word, "he causes my thoughts to become agreeable to His will."

Proverbs 16 opens with these words: "The preparations of the heart belong to man, but the answer of the tongue is from the Lord. All the ways of a man are pure in his own eyes, but the Lord weighs the spirits. Commit your works to the Lord, and your thoughts will be established."

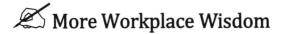 More Workplace Wisdom

Congratulations if you have completed praying 200 prayers. I pray that you will sense a new strength in your life and wisdom in your profession. The following pages are additional Workplace Wisdom devotions.

To continue to receive fresh new wisdom and insights, sign up for Marketplace Christians at

www.facebook.com/marketplacechristians

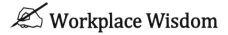 Workplace Wisdom

Alert and Oriented Times 4

"He who dwells in the secret place of the Most High shall remain stable and fixed under the shadow of the Almighty whose power no foe can withstand" (Psalm 91: 1).

Do you sense that something is about to happen in the World? Do you think there will be a crisis of some sort that will wake people up and bring them back to God? It is like a rumbling deep in the earth and in our spirits that we cannot explain.

I'm not fearful about it (read Psalm 91) – but I want to be prepared spiritually and financially to minister to others.

Our middle son was trained as an EMT and a paramedic firefighter. There is a quick evaluation they do on the patient to determine if he or she is alert and to what level the patient is oriented. They do this by looking in the eyes and asking questions.

A normal person is "Alert and Oriented Times 4." If the person cannot remember recent events, he or she is "Alert and Oriented Times 3." More disoriented – Times 2; drunk or in shock – Times 1; and a complete loss of identity is "Alert and Oriented Times 0."

We can use this measurement in our own lives with our emotions or spiritual reactions. A crisis can take us to a "3," "2," or "1" in the form of depression, loss of hope, low self-esteem, heart ache, or grief. A "0" means a complete loss of our identity and who we are in Christ.

I think the Lord wants to prepare us to be "Alert and Oriented Times 4" in time of crisis or emergency. If we do drop down – the proper training and preparation – we can quickly come back around. He wants us to recognize the attacks of the enemy, band together with our brothers and sisters, and fight the battle.

When our son takes a firefighter test, demonstrating his paramedic skills in front of a panel of evaluators, he finds himself in a state of "3" or "2" from the stress. He performs accurately, but he has occasionally been too slow and has to re-take the test.

However, in a REAL emergency on the job – everything always comes together for him. He is alert, accurate, fast, and saves lives. All his training and preparation produces a "4." Part of it is the adrenaline, but most of it is his focus on the person and years of experience and training.

In time of crisis, like adrenaline, the Holy Spirit will guide us – but we also need to be equipped and prepared – even if we have to re-take the test. Preparation comes with Word of God training – no other way. But we can remain "Alert and Oriented Times 4" if we "fix our eyes not on what is seen but on what is unseen" (2 Corinthians 4: 18).

In time of crisis at home or at work, you can give into your emotions of panic and fear, or you can train yourself to lean into God and draw from His strength, proclaiming His Word in the situation. A lot of people are going to depend on your calm, your peace, and your faith.

✍ Workplace Wisdom

Bluetooth Generation

"In a multitude of words, transgression is not lacking, but he who restrains his lips is prudent. The tongue of those who are upright and in right standing with God is as choice silver; the mind of those who are wicked and out of harmony with God is of little value" (Proverbs 10: 19 & 20, Amplified).

I travel frequently and I am in two to four airports a month. It is commonplace to see business people sitting in the gate area talking looking like they are talking to "no one." They are actually conducting business through their wireless phone ear piece – called a *Bluetooth*.

Almost every trip, there is a man pacing the floor and yelling at his girlfriend or wife about some detail that didn't get done or some attitude that he didn't like. Sometimes a business woman is yelling at a staff member. Everyone in the waiting area cringes and feels sorry for the person at the other end of his or her wrath. We sort of eye one another in amazement that someone actually talks this way to another human being and gets away with it.

I ask myself – what could make a sane, normal human being act this way? Could it be a missed flight, jet lag, financial stress to name a few? Or is it perhaps a controlling nature that is frustrated being away from home and losing control?

The workplace is becoming more and more stressful with shorter deadlines, fast paced decisions, and economic downfalls. I think the anger I see in the airport is the result of the world's pressure for financial success.

If the stress and anger destroys your peace, joy, family life and work relationships, then the prosperity and success you are trying to attain is actually making you poor.

We must keep God's perspective in these high pressure times. I believe when we meet our Maker, God will not ask how much money we made or what company we created – but He will rather ask, "How did you love?" How did you love the family and friends I gave you? How did you love others in your neighborhood or workplace?

As Jesus perfectly explains: "Do not gather and heap up for yourselves treasures on earth, where moth and rust corrupts, and where thieves break through and steal; but gather and heap up and store for yourselves treasures in heaven . . . For where your treasure is, there will you heart be also" (Matthew 6: 19 – 21, Amplified).

Do you use high pressure and stress as an excuse to be temperamental or unkind to someone? Instead of rationalizing or yielding over to self-indulging behavior, reflect on God's way of dealing with it and give the pressure over to Him. Trust God that if you put "first things first" in your behavior that everything else will be taken care of and fall in to place.

✍ Workplace Wisdom

Time Submits to the Master

". . . being confident of this very thing, that he who has begun a good work in you will complete it until the day of Jesus Christ." Philippians 1: 6

Did you know that Jesus was never in a hurry and He never was late? Everywhere He went, time and circumstances submitted to Him.

He always walked with purpose and toward a destination, and He never worried about His arrival time. Even when Martha and Mary thought He was too late to heal Lazarus, He was right on time to raise him from the dead (John 11:21).

Jesus is Lord of the universe and Lord of time. The Word says that a day is a thousand to the Lord (Psalm 90:4). God told Habakkuk that the vision "though it tarry" will not be one day late (Habakkuk 2:3).

This has a profound impact on my earthly perspective because it means that God can speed things up or slow things down in the spirit realm. No matter what we do, we cannot impact God's timetable. His Word says that He will complete what He began (Philippians 1:5-7).

What does this mean? It means I am to not waste time and continue to move forward; not fear time because "my times are in the Lord's hands" (Psalm 31: 15). It also means that the Lord can redeem the time whenever we may make a mistake with God's plan for our life.

In addition to planning, organizing, and keeping a time management system, I can make sure my compass is "pointed north" toward my Creator. I can commit my way to the Lord, and trust that He will direct my steps to the right place and in the right time.

My last major political assignment for the Lord was in Washington, D.C. as President of the *American Parents' Association*. The Lord told me in my heart and through others that I would be coming away for a season for training but to "not fear" because when it was time for me to go on the frontlines again I would pick things up as if I had not even been away. He said, "It would be like I had not missed one step in the plan."

That was 1991 when I received that message, and I have been in a training ground ever since obtaining experience in corporations, government, and education. I know when the call comes it will only be "one step" into that open door.

"Commit your way to the Lord. Trust also in Him, and He shall bring it to pass. He shall bring forth your righteousness as the light, and your justice as the noonday" (Psalm 37: 5 – 6).

 Workplace Wisdom

Imagination

Did you know that imagination is just a thought away from reality? Jesus knew the power of imagination, or He would not have used parables to make a point.

Famous inventions begin in the human imagination. When scientists and inventors use their imaginations to combine two existing perceptions, the result is a "synthesis." A synthesis combines two or more pre-existing elements resulting in the formation of something new.

Hewlett-Packard has provided consumers with many inventions that were synthesized through human imagination. After the invention of the calculator, engineers invented a calculator that printed paper. Later, several engineers determined in their imagination that the printing calculator could expand into a "large printing machine" to be used in conjunction with home computers.

Synthesis not only applies to inventions and technological advances. Synthesis also works as a spiritual concept: "combining the Word of God with our faith will result in the formation of what is in our imagination."

This puts a reality to the Hebrew message: "Now faith is the substance of things hoped for, the evidence of things not seen...By faith we understand that the worlds were framed by the Word of God, so that the things which are seen were not made of things which are visible" (Hebrews 11: 1 – 3).

If you have a dream in your heart – it started in your imagination. If you are not confessing your dream, then you don't believe it is real. You need to talk about it, pursue it, and envision details about it. You need to see yourself with it, meditate on it, and stick with it in order for it to come to pass.

I am not suggesting you just make-up anything in your imagination. I am suggesting that dreams and visions come to us through our imaginations, and we dismiss them as not being real. The dream, inspiration, or heart's desire was more than likely planted as a seed from the Lord, but we dismissed because it seemed foolish or impossible.

Inventors at the 3M Company often have more faith in their imaginations than Christians have in the promises of God. When they get an idea, similar to Edison and the light bulb, they do not give up. They pursue the vision with tests and trials over and over again until it becomes a reality.

The company *3-M* (inventors of Scotch Tape and Post-It Notes) has an interesting philosophy for their inventors:

"Conceive, believe, achieve. Persistence—combined with creativity and faith—is still the best formula for long-term success. Don't let one approach or solution blind you to better options. Struggle is a necessary component of success. Patient money and patient people help the big ideas germinate. Ask your customers what quality is—then never let the standard slip."

Are you ready to conceive, believe, and achieve?

"Now to Him who is able to do exceedingly abundantly above all that we ask or think, according to the power that works in us" (Ephesians 3: 20).

About the Author

Dr. Wendy Flint, national speaker, has over 30-years' experience in the marketplace from entry level employee, to elected official, to supervisor and manager, to corporate executive. She is author of ten books and training manuals for business, government, and education.

Dr. Flint is a former tenured professor from a community college in California, served as adjunct faculty at Biola University and is an online instructor at Central Christian College of Kansas. She teaches business, principles of management and organizational leadership courses.

Dr. Flint is currently Chief Learning Officer for a non-profit education organization. She trains faculty in learner-centered classrooms, integrating technology and workplace skills across the curriculum.

Wendy and her husband Terry of 46 years, currently reside in Portland, Oregon and have three children and six grandchildren. Wendy also became an "American Mom," sponsor, and mentor for a Christian student from Ivory Coast Africa. He is now an American citizen and his family is now her family, and she is "Nana" to his son.

Dr. Flint holds a Masters of Public Administration, a Masters of Business Administration, and a PhD in Education with a specialization in teaching and learning.

www.marketplacechristians.com

www.drwendyflint.com

www.linkedin.com/in/drwendyflint

Other Works by Dr. Wendy Flint

Instructional Excellence for Health Professionals (Training Manual)

MarketplaceChristians.com (Book Amazon)

Principled and Practical Leadership (Training Manual)

Prison Prayers: Give Us Our Daily Bread (Book Amazon)

Problem-based Learning: Welcome to the Real World (Book Amazon)

School Boards – A Call to Action (Book Out of Print)

Teaching Techniques for Adult Learners (Training Manual)

The Parents Right to Know (Book Out of Print)

21st Century Student Leadership Skills (Training Manual)

Made in the USA
Middletown, DE
10 January 2020